Black Women

FOR BEGINNERS

WRITERS AND READERS PUBLISHING, INCORPORATED

P.O. Box 461, Village Station
New York, NY 10014

c/o Airlift Book Company
26 Eden Grove
London N7 8EF
England

A Writers and Readers Documentary Comic Book
Copyright © 1993
Library of Congress Catalog Card Number 91-050562
ISBN # 0-86316-152-9 Cloth
ISBN # 0-86316-147-2 Trade
1 2 3 4 5 6 7 8 9 0

Manufactured in the United States of America

Beginners Documentary Comic Books are published by Writers and Readers Publishing, Inc. Its trademark, consisting of the words "For Beginners, Writers and Readers Documentary Comic Books" and the Writers and Readers logo, is registered in the U. S. Patent and Trademark Office and in other countries.

Black Women
FOR BEGINNERS

NEW YORK • LONDON

ACKNOWLEDGEMENTS

I would not have had the courage to tackle this expansive subject without the knowledge, wisdom and blessings of my Historical Consultants, the beloved Dr. John Henrik Clarke and the passionate scholar Runoko Rashidi. In addition, Special Thanks is due:

to Errol Sauti Collier for census and statistical research, Nailah Lee Randall for French translations, Yemi Touré and Ron Wilkins, international affairs consultants;

to my enthusiastic, persistent research assistants: Amy Holloway, Dionne Bennett, Carol Moreno, Marq Hawkins, Felicia Howell and Estella Holman;

to my international contributors: Natalie Asfaha and Katharina Oguntoye in Germany, James Patterson and Lily Golden in Russia, Andy Reese Maddox and Sylvia Blanco-Green in Australia, Nadia Raveles in Surinam, June Giovanni, Kwesi Owusu and Menelik Shabazz in London, Regina Dominquez and Silvana Afram in Brazil, and Kouka Honore Queadrago in Burkina Faso;

to Dr. Daniel T. Williams, Tuskegee U's archivist, Miriam Jiminez Roman and Betty Odibasian at the Schomburg, Reynaldo Reyes at the United Nations Photo Library, and a host of persevering librarians across the country;

to professors/authors Rhonda Cobham, Edward Scobie, Atty. LeGrand Clegg, Elaine Armour, Toni Trives and Carlos Guillermo (Cubena) Williams for sharing their research;

to collectors Charles L. Blockson, Rudy Calvo, Atty. LeGrand Clegg, John E. Collins, Cecil Fergerson, Janette Faulkner, Alden Kimbrough, Sarah and George Livingston, Tsan Merritt-Poree, Stanley Nelson, Lorraine Raglin and James Wheeler for sharing their stuff;

to Women Make Movies distribution co-op in New York for giving me access to films on Black women from around the world, and to Ada Griffin and Michelle Parkerson of Third World Newsreel for sharing transcripts from their film-in-progress;

to my manuscript readers: Elaine Armour, Cheryl Chisholm, D. Jean Collins, Arabella Chavers-Julien, Eric Cyrs, Imani Douglas and Raymond Shields, who challenged me to write it right;

to Beverly Hall, whose wonderful artwork rekindled my enthusiasm;

to the early historians J.A. Rogers, Chancellor Williams, Cheikh Anta Diop and Drucilla Dunjee Houston who did the hard part;

and to all those not listed here who opened the path by sending materials, encouragement and returning my phone calls.

Saundra

CONTENTS

*"I am travelling on a
spiritual mission,
but sometimes
I get distracted."*

The Unborn Child
Julie Dash (USA)

For my young Sistuh friends
who are at their beginnings.

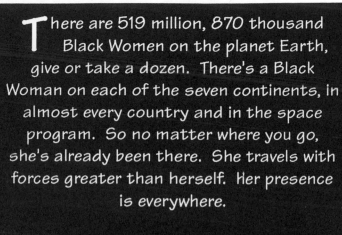

There are 519 million, 870 thousand Black Women on the planet Earth, give or take a dozen. There's a Black Woman on each of the seven continents, in almost every country and in the space program. So no matter where you go, she's already been there. She travels with forces greater than herself. Her presence is everywhere.

The BW* is the African Diaspora in its highest feminine form.

Spotlight, please —

She is so bodacious that, here at the head of the 21st Century, other folks are now claiming to **be** her.

So from the git-go:
Black is not just other than White.
Black is more than the experience of Oppression.
Black is exactly that.

And while we accept the recognition of Others as a compliment, we think the Black Woman has earned her own space, that space is sacred, and we dare to claim that space for her.

With all due respect, and with the understanding that there is no monolithic Black Woman, we're going to use these abbreviated I.D.'s as our shorthand:

BW = Black Woman   **BWn** = Black Women

BWs = Black Woman's or Women's (possessive)

WHERE DID SHE COME FROM?

(AND THEN, WHERE
DID SHE GO??)

We thought you'd never ask!

The BW comes from Africa, which holds (to date) the only evidence of humans living more than a million years ago. Her most famous known ancestor is "Lucy" ...

... whose skeleton was at least 3 million years old when they tripped over it in an Ethiopian desert back in 1974. What a surprise! However, Lucy hadn't finished evolving into a "Human" as we know them today. That took another 2 million, 800 hundred thousand (or so) years.

Which brings us to the first known diva,
SISTUH EVE— our "Mitochondrial Mother,"
or _cell_ mother.

sistuh Eve

Through modern technology, scientists have isolated the DNA
in our gene cells, and determined that a Sistuh (whom they nick-
named "Eve") lived some 200,000 years ago, (roughly 6 million
years post chimpanzee), claimed Africa as her hometown, and liked
to travel. Which is to say, scientifically, that everybody came from
one woman, and she was Black.

Black!!
black
b-l-a-c-k

Of course, not everyone is thrilled about this:

This bone proves that she is one million years old.

This DNA cell proves she's 200,000 years old, and...**Black**!

This Bible says she's 6,000 years old... and... blonde?

Who wrote that?

Mohenjo

Still, Sistuh Eve represents the beginning of **modern** homo sapiens, modern **"humans"** — folks who walk, eat, and reason like you do, and that's what's important. She is the original "First Lady."

Aunt Viola?
Deaconess Jones?

No, this
Mohenjo-Daro
bronze image
dates back to
the Harappan
people of
2500 B.C.

The woman made a career out of grandmothering. She's the great-great-great-great-great-great-great-great-great-grea — whoops! — we're out of room.... O.K.!, she's the great grandmother 100 squared of us all. Everybody has an Eve connection.

So, how did this African diva turn some of her children white???

WHERE DID SHE GO?

Sistuh Eve and her children went all over the place, via migration, war, commerce, assimilation, enslavement, marriage, procreation. They took their melanin (the genetic stuff that keeps them bbbBlack) with them.

In ancient times Africa and Asia were connected by land, so Sistuh Eve sent some of her children out to play—-in what we know today as Asia, India, Europe and the Americas.

Around 5000 years ago some families moved from Africa to Sumer (in Southwest Asia, later known as Mesopotamia). A few hundred years later the DRAVIDIANS went to check out the Indus Valley (India), stayed, and ruled it for a thousand years. Today India has the largest number of Blacks in Asia.

A modern Dravidian woman, early 1900's.

Another Black prehistoric group, the GRIMALDIS, made it to Europe some 30,000 to 40,000 years ago, and are considered its first modern population. (If they'd known about the Ice Age they would have stayed home.) Their icons have been discovered in Italy and Australia.

A 4½" clay piece by the Grimaldis, one of the earliest depictions of the female form. Found in Austria, dubbed (strangely) "The Venus of Willendorf."

The Anu (Ani) people from Southern Europe and Nubia settled in China, India and Persia (now Iran), and Blacks were visible in China's Shang Dynasty from 1766 - 1043 B.C.

"Negritos whom the Chinese call 'Black Dwarfs' are reported in the mountainous districts south of Yangtze ... Some emigrated, but others remained and were assimilated by the dominant southern Mongolian stock, as witness to kinky hair and swarthy skin noticeable among a few southern Chinese."

L. Carrington Goodrich
A Short History Of The Chinese People, (USA)

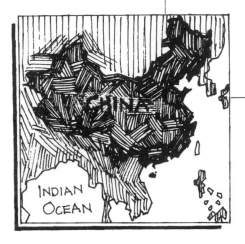

INDIAN
OCEAN

As documented by Herodotus and others, Blacks (Colchians) have been in Russia for at least 3000 years, near the Black Sea in the Caucaucus Mountains. In the late 17th Century, Blacks were imported by Peter the Great as servants and court amusements.

Around 1000 B.C. sailors from Africa's southwest coast (Guinea) made boats and followed the ocean currents to the Americas. Their self-portraits--stone heads averaging 7' tall, weighing 20 tons--have been found throughout Mexico and Central America.

A 20 ton artifact should make you wonder how anyone could celebrate Chris Columbus' "discovery!"

The Italian navigator Amerigo Vespucci was headed toward the Americas in 1500 when (according to his letters) he spotted Black men on the Caribbean island that is now Curacao. He later witnessed African sailors on the Atlantic **returning** to Africa.

In other words, the BW's presence outside Africa began, not as a slave, but free!

HOW LONG WERE THEY GONE?

Long enough for Sistuh Eve's children to change their physical appearance. Sistuh Eve's descendants provided the seed for all the non-Black populations known today.

Over hundreds of years they adapted to different climates, terrains, foods, etc., with slow changes they didn't even notice. But moms see everything, and when they came home again—to trade or to conquer or to get some clean laundry—Sistuh Eve saw that some of her children's hair had straightened out. Their eyes had narrowed. Their physique had changed. They were low on melanin so they were looking a little bleached, or a little yellow, or, my goodness!, even white.

So now there
were races
distinguished by color.
and...
humans had discovered
the art of
SEXUAL POLITICS:

a) the **SEXUAL** part:
Conquerors slept with the
folks they conquered.
Travelers slept with the folks
they visited. This took the
BW around the world more
"intimately" than anything.
(In time, women who were
despised for their race would
be wooed, wedded and
bedded by "the enemy.")

What did
you say your
name was?

b) the **POLITICS**
part: In "Dynastic
incest" queens mar-
ried their brothers
and cousins to pre-
serve the family
power line. **Gender,**
even without sex,
was manipulated in
political relation-
ships to secure land
for **empires.**
EMPIRE BUILDING!
Ah, there's the rub!....

Sistuh Eve's children were into DYNASTIES long before the TV show (and did it better!)

During B.C., empire building was relatively local. A few conquerings here, a few dynasties there. Africa was invaded for the first time in the 1700's B.C. by the Hyksos, a people the Egyptians had formerly ruled. The Greeks came en masse to Egypt (which **is** in Africa) where they learned all the stuff they later claimed to have created on their own. However, as we cross the bridge into the Christian Era, things get a lot more complicated.

EMPIRE BUILDING

In the mid 1600's, there was an Irish invasion (well, in a manner of speaking) of Jamaica:

AMANDA CASH ROMAN
b. approx. 1840, a Black American whose Jamaican mother married a Jamaican Irishman.

Oliver Cromwell sent a large group of Irish prisoners to…Jamaica [where] they intermarried with blacks…and over a period of years lost their identity. Today many black Jamaicans still carry Irish surnames.

— Joseph John Williams
Whence the "Black Irish" of Jamaica (USA)

In 711 those handsome Moors went all the way to Europe to conquer Spain. Then they missed that home cooking and sent for their women. Black men and women ruled Spain for seven centuries, imprinting the literature, architecture and culture.

"In the Portuguese runs a deep current of Negro blood, and there the Negro has often risen to the caste of the nobility. Napoleon's army had many small, black Portugese soldiers...merchants purchased...Negroes as servants; in all large cities of commerce there were several hundred blacks, and many a house was known simply as 'at the Moors'."

Brunold Springer,
Racial Mixture
As The Basic Principle Of Life
(Germany 1940)

Which is how we came to have Black
blood among the royalty of Europe...

QUEEN CHARLOTTE
SOPHIA, 1744-1818
German-born wife of
England's George III.
(Described by court
observer Walpole as "Not
a beauty, the nostrils
spreading too wide; mouth
has the same fault."
(Of course!)

...and vice versa:

TSAN MERRITT-PORRE,
a bona fide Black
Jew, and her
German-Jewish great-
grandmother,
Elizabeth Cohen-
Johnston. Tsan, a
culinary arts special-
ist, "keeps Kosher" in
her home.

(I know this is a little rough on some of you, so go make a cup of tea, stay calm
and stay tuned.)

Exploration = *a Hard Time*
Colonialism = *a Bad Time*
Slavery = *for a Long Time*

Imagine going to the market and finding out
that YOU are the item on sale.

Starting in the late
1300's the BW was
taken on a 500-year
world tour without
tourist status.

She was taken from West Africa to the West Indies to be "trained" for slavery, then dispatched to the United States to do her j.o.b.

She was taken by Arabs from East Africa to Turkey and other slave centers around the Black Sea.

She was taken to Jamaica where she fought enslavement for a century. Dubbed a Maroon, she was captured in the late 1700's and shipped to Nova Scotia.

In 1517 she was used to entice Spaniards to settle in Latin America. "Have slaves, will go."

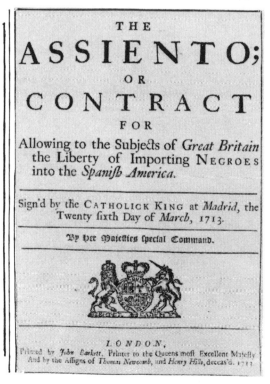

This 1713 treaty allowed British control of the slave trade in Latin America.

She was sent to the Dominican Republic, Brazil, Surinam, Cuba, to cut sugar cane and refine it for European tastes.

"The Chinese ravished New Guinea for slaves. By the 14th, 15th Century, the Muslim-Indonesian Sultan of Pidor was going to New Guinea for slaves for the Middle East, Turkey and Iraq, and for exportation to the Chinese empire."

C. Madang,
"The African Diaspora In Asia"

She was taken from the Sudan, Libya and Chad to Yugoslavia. Descendants could be found in Ulcinj as recently as the 1950's.

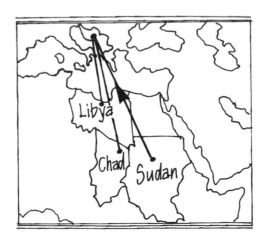

Only the money was counted, not the victims. So the numbers on slavery are not in yet. But historians' wide-ranging estimates show from 5 to 30 million BWn taken from Africa.

1796 drawing by Stedman documented a slave's beating in Surinam.

After all that, some Sistuhs actually got back to Africa. In 1787 Maroons and Black Loyalists who were suffering in Nova Scotia accepted Britain's offer to be returned to Sierra Leone.

Between 1820 and 1870 hundreds of Blacks from the Americas and West Indies voluntarily moved to Liberia, sponsored by "colonization societies."

Not all Blacks during the period of slavery were slaves.

Captured Africans survived the wreck of Spanish ships off the Caribbean coast of St. Vincent in 1635, and formed a community with the Carib Indians and slave fugitives from other islands.

In the U.S., Indians (Native Americans) assisted escaped slaves. Through intermarriage a substantial group of free "Black Indians" evolved.

"The number of Afro-Americans with an Indian ancestor was once estimated at about one-third of the total. In Latin America the percentage is much higher."

William Loren Katz,
Black Indians (USA)

Diana Fletcher, a Black Indian of the Kiowa Nation.

Loyalists were those siding with Britain during America's war for independence. Among them were free Blacks and Blacks who gained freedom in exchange for soldiering. Some 5,000 fled to Canada. More followed after the War of 1812. In the early 1900's Black families founded settlements in Alberta and Saskatchewan.

MARY SEACOLE, an adventurous nurse, was born in Jamaica, schooled in Britain, nursed cholera victims in Panama with her own formula. In the mid 1850's she found her way to Turkey, setting up a mini-hospital and canteen for soldiers in the Crimean War. She was celebrated in England as a war hero.

"Some people have called me
quite a female Ulysses. They intended it as
a compliment but from my experience of
the Greeks, I do not consider
it a very flattering one."

Through the trade of goods, the African presence in Germany predates colonialism. After WWI the occupation forces brought their colonized African soldiers to Germany. Black men and German women produced daughters who became victims of the Nazi regime.

"We often heard about mulattoes being taken to concentration camps... Many colored women were sterilized. Christel's mother hid her in a convent near Cologne. They got her out of there and sterilized her too. Our nephew, also."

Doris Reiprich and Erike Ngambi ul Kuo, *Farbe Bekennen (Showing Our Colors)* (Germany)

1990 photo of German BWn includes three generations of one family.

Estimates of today's Afro-German population, where there is no longer a census by race, range from 30 thousand to one million.

"Where did she go?"
is a question some Sistuhs hope **no** one **ever** answers.

We tried to get some first-hand interviews.
Skin color and assumptions have destroyed the unity of Black communities world-wide.

We put an ad in the paper.
The "one- 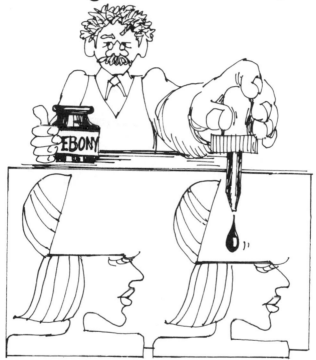 -of-black-blood" theory––

...created The Mulatto, the Quadroon, the Octoroon, the...

We asked for referrals.
The 🝆 has cost millions in "miscegenation" litigation and legislation from S.A. to U.S.A., while filling the coffers of Hollywood.

We stood on corners taking notes.
The 🝆 has caused much stress and heartbreak among those who want one 🝆 and those who want to get rid of the one 🝆 they have.

We staked out family reunions and stores selling bleaching creams.

Assimilation = a marked decline in the African-descended populations of several Central and South American countries. Brazil has the largest number of Blacks living outside Africa, yet in Brazil's 1980 census only 5.7% (7.5 million) of the citizens claimed to be "Black."

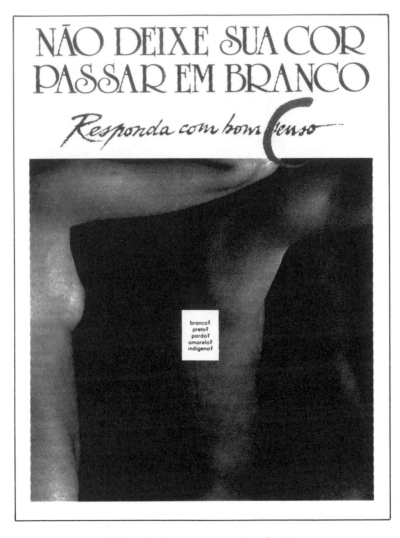

"Don't let your color fade into white/Don't let yourself be erased."

Brazilian Census poster

We eavesdropped
on old wives telling tales.

You have to marry lighter and lighter, then the race will disappear.

None of the Sistuhs who are currently "passing" would agree to be interviewed for this book.

We wanted to tell them that if one 💧 could make your whole thang truly Black, then perhaps it's one hell of a powerful 💧 , which may be the real reason we've been forced to share it, and maybe they should rethink this.

Translation on 1924 North African post card reads "Woman of Chad—white race"

Oh, really?!

"Ancient black life rooted upon its base with all its fascinating new layers of brown, low-brown, high-brown, nut-brown, lemon, maroon, olive, mauve, gold. Yellow balancing between black and white. Black reaching out beyond yellow. Almost-white on the brink of change. Sucked back down into the current of black by the terribly sweet rhythm of black blood..."

photo: Jacqueline Alexander

Claude McKay, *Home To Harlem* (Jamaica)

"Young Black Woman
what's your name?

. . . .

It's pride and beauty
For I have no shame
I'm Young Black Woman.
You know my name."

Sebek Sanyika
(USA)

Folks can't handle something without a name.

Names that denote status, race, physical look, free or slave, and especially names with attitudes.

The BW was **renamed** after being "discovered" by colonialists. A slave's name was often changed when she was sold, making it difficult to reunite with family or to maintain a personal identity. With freedom, some declared their names invalid — "slave names"— and took one of their own liking.

Ngungalari.

"Keep your
Nellie Strongfellow
for Ngungalari is
my name.
I am last and lost in
this strange land
that once
was mine."

Archie Weller (Australia)

NELLIE

Names become part of
social rituals—who can
call who what, and get
away with it.

Names can put you in boxes (class x caste x category x character). Or they can clarify. ▼

"I'm a Black Feminist Lesbian Mother Warrior Poet."

Audre Lorde (USA)

Naming should not be confused
with name-calling. To help you
distinguish, we offer:

NAMES BY WHICH SHE IS KNOWN

A GLOSSARY

African queen - a head-up BW of the African diaspora

auntie - 1) masters'/overseers' name for female slave who can no
longer breed; 2) member of your extended (non-blood) family
who loves you like you were her own

Aunt Jemima - one of the most recognized
symbols of the happy "mammy," used
to market pancakes and other
domestic products to Whites since
the 1880's. The name Jemimah once
had esteem as the eldest of Job's
(the Bible) daughters, and as a city in ancient Arabia
named after its queen

Auset (Ast) - original, Egyptian name for Isis

baby - an affectionate ID for a lover, friend or kin

beef - Jamaican males' description of a BW

bellywoman - a pregnant West Indian woman

bleke-uma - a BW in Surinam

black rose, black pearl - poetic
descriptions of the BW

blonde Negroid - term coined by
European historians
to describe Europeans
with a **visible** "Negro strain"
(broad nose, thick lips); a.k.a.
Nordic Negro

London edition of the
American song, 1831

NEW EDITION.
Life in Philadelphia
or the
COAL BLACK ROSE.

Lubly Rosa, Sambo Cum.

Sung by
Mr WEBSTER,

breeder - a slave forced into multiple pregnancies to increase the number of slave laborers

Candace - translation of ancient Ethiopian word for Kentake, a female ruler

chamba - A Black West Indian woman in Panama, often used negatively in Latin American countries

Cleopatra - reference point, as in "the Cleopatra of _____"; applied to very sensuous BWn, particularly if they have a good head for business

cocola - a Black West Indian woman in the Dominican Republic

daughter - an affectionate I.D., no age or family relationship required

Angela Davis - reference point, as in "the Angela Davis of_____"; applied to tall, politically outspoken BWn. Around the world in 1970, sistuhs were arrested for "being" Angela, even after she was incarcerated

diva - BW who gives a consistently strong performance, with or without a stage/audience

Eve - 1) scientists' nickname denoting the first modern homosapiens; 2) in theology, the mother of all living humans, but also the first alleged transgressor

> **"Then we started to think about how we should name ourselves. Some people didn't understand the expression Afro-German and we had to define it together again. [1980's]**
>
> Katharina Oguntoye,
> Initiative of Black Germans
> (Germany)

exotic erotic - some folks' fantasy psychosis which sees all Black women as simultaneously strange, fascinating, primal and childlike, uninhibited, earthy, sensuous and highly sexed. ("You can be some of the women all of the time, but you can't be all...")

gin - British colonizers' term for native Aboriginal woman

Hey, mama! - 1) a warm greeting 2) a catch phrase used by unfamiliar men, usually followed by "Can I go wich choo?"

ho - a derivative of, but less operative than, "whore", since you don't have to <u>be</u> one to be called one

hot chocolate - a very sexy BW

Isis - 1) the mother/ruler, most popular goddess in ancient mythology 2) a computer data base, described as: "a stand-alone... management system. Functions include ordering, claiming, check-in, routing, loan control and fund accounting.... When stuck, press HELP key, and Isis will tell you exactly what to do." (If the crown fits, claim it.)

light Egyptian - a make-up color used on White actresses hired to play Black women

Lucy - three-million-year-old skeleton found in Ethiopia in 1974, named by archeologists for a Beatles' song

mama - 1) birth mother 2) catch-all I.D. for a BW who is anything **but** the biological mother of the caller, often preceded by "pretty," "little" or "sweet"

"When you call me Mama Do you see my Woman?...

Carole Stewart (Britain)

mambo - a female priestess of Vodoun (Haiti)

mammy - a BW who suckles and cares for White children, usually at the expense of her own

matriarch - 1) historically, a woman in a social system where kinship and power are handed down through the female; redefined pejoratively as a woman who runs a household or business without a male partner and is therefore assumed to be domineering. 2) a family's female elder

my house - a contemporary possession name, used by men to describe the BW they live with. Similar names include: "my crib," "my nest"

"My father always had the greatest admiration for the German people and their industrial achievements. That's why he insisted on that terrible name 'Winifred,' which became 'Winnie.' ...It is a constant reminder of our oppression! My African name 'Nomzamo' means in Xhosa 'trial' --- those that in their life will go through many trials..."

Winnie Mandela, *Part Of My Soul Went With Him*, (South Africa)

negress - feminine form of "negro." Usage today could get you in trouble

prike - a BW in Surinam (Tonga language)

Queen mother - esteemed elder BW in the community

Queen of the Nile - an honorary title bestowed on today's BW to remind her of her royal history before Affirmative Action and MTV and "fly girls"

Rock of Gibraltar - an analogy to the BW's legendary, everlasting strength in the face of everything

sapphire - 1) from the Hebrew "Sapphira," a precious stone metaphysically representing Truth and that which is beautiful; 2) a sassy BW who calls it like it is. Usually seen with her hand on her hip even when it isn't

sistuh/ sister/ sista - the most popular I.D. for a BW

Harriet Tubman - reference point, as in "the Harriet Tubman of_____"; a BW who gets the job done despite all odds

> Brooklyne, October 29, 1787
> Dear Sir:
> I have taken the liberty at the desire of my father of sending to your care a Negro wench named Eve and her child named Sukey in order to dispose of them to the best advantage. She is an excellent hand at all sorts of house work except cooking, and one of the best servants for washing we ever had; she is perfectly honest and sober and the only fault she has is being near sighted. Mr. Francis Pemart and his daughter Mrs. Stoothoff, Mr. Thomas Horsfield and family and Mr. John Guest know the wench and can prove the property...

1787 slave letter, selling a slave named Eve from New York to Canada

yaaya - an old woman, word preserved from the Bantu languages

---

The slave Belle renamed herself "Sojourner" for the path she had chosen, and "Truth" for her mission.

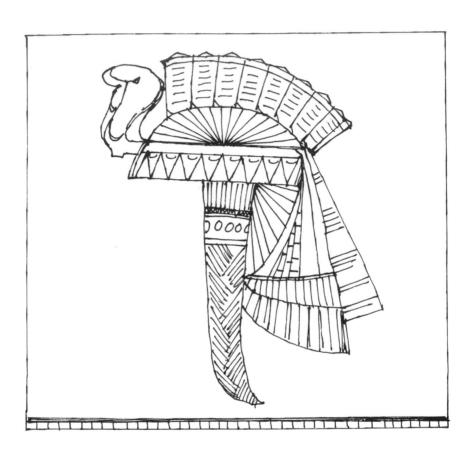

"Beauty is here because I am here."

17th century
Dutch woman

Quick! Who are the 5 most famous Black Women in the world today?? (Living.)

Unh-huh ....

The BW is an enigma. Even when famous.

"a perplexing, baffling, or seemingly inexplicable person/ see mystery"

H er mystery is
tucked into
his/story.

Sculpture of Egyptian princess,
approximately 2000 B.C.

The BW is the original IMAGE.
To decorate the body she created the first
earring, and the sandal.

12th century B.C.

(Earrings were also worn by men.)

She used earth and plants to create the first make-up.

South African Bushwomen made a skin "moisturizer" of animal fat mixed with clay.

To protect the eyes from glare she rubbed indigo and copper on her lids.

Oh, Oh!

Her influence on hair is world-wide.

International star Josephine Baker made the "pony tail" *the* hair style of the 1950's.

Some of her hair-
styles are 6000
years old.

Postage stamps
portraying
authentic hairstyles
from Gabon,
Central African
Republic, Burkina
Faso, Tikar woman
of Cameroun,
and Mandara
woman of
Cameroun, stamp
issued for the 1939
World's Fair.

"You could tell the clan, the village,
by the style of hair they wore…
Then the Yoruba people
were wearin' thirty braids or more…
You would know the princess, queen and bride
by the number of the braid
You would know the gods they worshipped
by the pattern that they made…"

Camille Yarbrough
(USA)

To protect the head from the sun, she designed the first wigs, visible on many early artifacts.

Queen Tiye, 1300's B.C., in Nubian style wig.

"Artificial hair, arranged in layers or tiers, [is] a style still seen in Black Africa. A hair-do worn by girls is called djimbi; slightly modified and worn by married women, it is called djere... In Egypt, the use of such wigs was popular with all social classes."

Cheikh Anta Diop,
African Origin Of Civilization, 1974
(Senegal)

djimbi

Scarification (cicatrization) is the original "body language": a painful process of pricking the skin, filling the wound and forcing it to scar. The resulting designs have specific social meanings but also immunize the body from some diseases, similar to a vaccination. It's still a popular practice throughout the world.

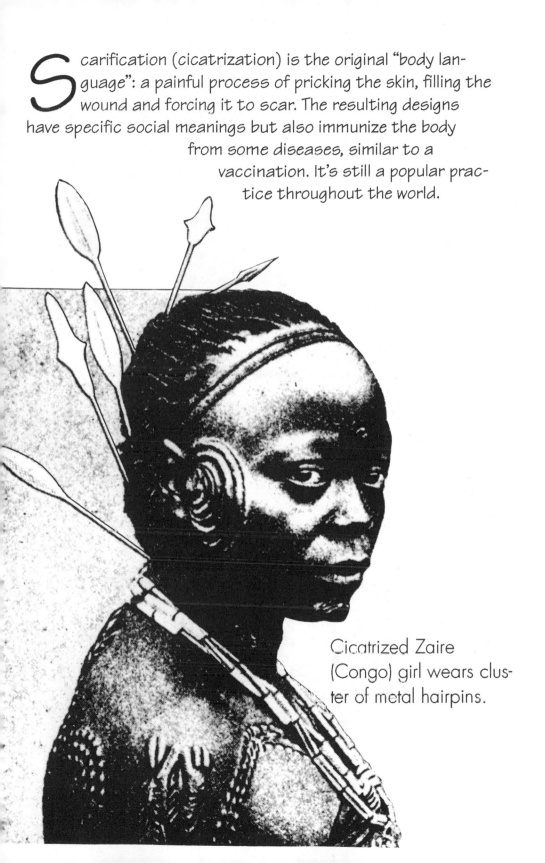

Cicatrized Zaire (Congo) girl wears cluster of metal hairpins.

To care for the spirit, she developed
the use of oils and perfumes. Today
it's called aromatherapy.

wall carving, Egyptian
women making perfume

To stimulate the mind
she studied the
mysteries, taught
philosophy, ran
governments, kept
libraries and served as
priestess.

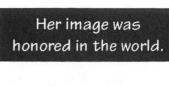

◄ 1931 French magazine cover, "Une Noire Vaut Deux Blancs" (One Black Woman Is Worth Two Whites)

"Alas I melt as wax ► at the sight of her beauty. She is Black, it is true, but what matters? Coals are black; but when they are alight they glow like rose cups."

Asclepiades, 270 B.C. (Greece)

Despite all this, the BW has an IMAGE problem. It's been usurped, manipulated, exalted, degraded, altered, exploited, suppressed and turned back against her.

Things have been so bad that a lot of sistuhs just gave up, went on over and adopted somebody else's Image.

Now why would she do **that**??

Because the "INFERIOR RACE" idea was created, with one race (who shall remain nameless but whose initials are W.P.) claiming to be supreme, via intellect and ability, with the god-given right to rule the "inferior" race.

Because men rewriting the Bible (again) changed "I am black **and** comely" to "black **but** comely," (Song of Solomon) and signed her name. Like Makeda needed to apologize!

> "We must not forget that the biblical authors were not writing history—they were creating religion. The Bible was not written by historians but by priests; and what they wrote was a statement of faith—not a statement of fact."

Savina J. Teubal, *Hagar The Egyptian* (USA)

Because she misplaced her reflection.

Because with the exploration and rape of Africa, Image took on some new colors:

Dark = **Ugly**	Light = Beauty
Black = **Evil**	White = Virtue

White actress Lillian Leighton in blackface.

''When we say 'we people,' we always mean we white people. The non-mention of color <u>always</u> implies pure white. What else could I mean?''

character in George Washington Cable's *The Grandissimes*, 1860

"Nothing makes a Negro's mouth water like a luscious, fresh-picked melon. Any colored "mammy" can hold a huge slice in one hand while holding her offspring in the other... What melons the Negroes do not consume will find favor with the pigs."

Life Magazine, August, 1937

Trinidadian JANELLE PENNY COMMISSIONG, the first BW crowned "Miss Universe" (1978), was frequently challenged about the validity of a BW representing the beauty standard for all the world's women.

The BW became immune to her Self and susceptible to Others.

IMAGE MACHINE

mammy	entertainer
Aunt Jemima	sexual primitive/whore
tragic mulatto	modern feminist "bitch"

Others took her mothering skills and turned her into a MAMMY.

Mammy Yams

LOUISIANA PORTO RICAN

SWEET POTATOES

PACKED BY
C. M. DEVALCOURT
S U N S E T
LOUISIANA
PRODUCE OF U.S.A.
50 LBS. NET

LOUISIANA
TAM SWEET
POTATOES

"The matriarch of the
    weak and young,
The lazy crooning, com-
        forting tongue.
She has children of
        her own
But the white-skinned ones
        are bone of her
        bone.
They may not be hers, but
        she is theirs...
Half a nuisance and half a
        mother
And legally neither one
        nor the other..."

Stephen Vincent Benet
(USA)

" To Mammy
Caroline Barr
Mississippi 1840-1940

Who was born in slavery and who gave
to my family a fidelity without stint or calculation
of recompense...."

William Faulkner,
dedication to Go Down
Moses, 1940 (USA)

◄Mammy: USA, 18__
/Germany, 1991 ▼

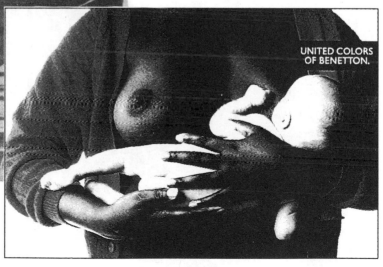

UNITED COLORS
OF BENETTON.

Aunt J., 1890 to 1990. Nancy Green, an ex-slave from Kentucky, was the first Aunt Jemima.

CLOTEL;

OR,

THE PRESIDENT'S DAUGHTER:

A Narrative of Slave Life

IN

THE UNITED STATES.

BY

WILLIAM WELLS BROWN,

A FUGITIVE SLAVE, AUTHOR OF "THREE YEARS IN EUROPE."

With a Sketch of the Author's Life.

"We hold these truths to be self-evident: that all men are created equal; that they are endowed by their Creator with certain inalienable rights, and that among these are LIFE, LIBERTY, and the PURSUIT OF HAPPINESS."—*Declaration of American Independence.*

LONDON:
PARTRIDGE & OAKEY, PATERNOSTER ROW;
AND 70, EDGWARE ROAD.
1853.

"...
girls
first time a white man
opens his fly
like a good thing
we'll just laugh
laugh real loud my
black women..."

Lucille Clifton
(USA)

PROGRAMME

THE OCTOROON

Dion Boucicault

First performed at the Winter Garden Theatre, New York on December 6, 1859.*

GEORGE PEYTON	JACKSON
SALEM SCUDDER	OLD PETE
MR. SUNNYSIDE	PAUL, *a boy slave*
JACOB M'CLOSKY	SOLON
WAHNOTEE	MRS. PEYTON
LAFOUCHE	ZOE
CAPTAIN RATTS	DORA SUNNYSIDE
COLONEL POINTDEXTER	GRACE
JULES THIBODEAUX	MINNIE
JUDGE CAILLOU	DIDO

THE LOVE STORY OF A GIRL WHO PASSED FOR WHITE!

This Year the Picture is

Pinky

Starring
JEANNE CRAIN · ETHEL BARRYMORE
ETHEL WATERS · WILLIAM LUNDIGAN

"Mulatismo"

They captured her style, bottled it and sold it back to her.

Nigerian "Barbie Doll" created by Mattel Toys in 1990 for adult doll collectors.

Grace Jones in German car ad

The BW was very confused. **On the one hand she was invisible:**

The French artist Bartholdi originally designed the Statue of Liberty as France's tribute to the emancipation of U.S. slaves. She had Negroid features and the broken chains of slavery hanging from her arm. He was encouraged to alter the image.

"Those people who are descendants of Africans and who were imported into this country and sold as slaves were not intended to be included under the word 'Citizens' in the Constitution…"

Chief Justice Taney, U.S. Supreme Court, rendering the 1857 Dred Scott decision

On the other
hand, she was all
over the place.

15c

EXPOSITION
COLONIALE
INTERNATIONALE

PARIS
1931

POSTES

"Sanrio company came under
fire after reports surfaced that
it was marketing a line of "Little Black Sambo" toys in
Japan...Sambo and his sister,
Hanna, with very black faces,
large white eyes and other
exaggerated physical features."

Los Angeles Times
December 23, 1988

Postage stamps for
France's Colonial
Exposition, Paris, 1931.

Coco-cola advt tray, "The Wedding"

Fashion models
Beverly Johnson and Iman

Nairobi's
edition of Viva

The "Italian Cleopatra," Anna dei Medici, on jewelled
candle holder kept in the Louvre

It was like owning a bank but not
being able to get any credit.

MISS AMERICAS

"What's wrong with this picture?"

"What W.E.B. DuBois called double
consciousness, 'this sense of always looking at one's
self through the eyes of others, of measuring one's
soul by the tape of a world that looks on in
amused contempt and pity,' creates its own
particular kind of disfigurement in the lives of black
women... far more than the external facts and
figures of oppression, the true terror is within; the
mutilation of the spirit <u>and</u> the body."

Mary Helen Washington,
Sturdy Black Bridges (USA)

The results of this life-threatening assault on the spirit can be psychoanalyzed until Freud reincarnates, but basically it shows up as:

LIPS, HIPS and HAIR!

The BW dispersed outside the motherland was told she was not pretty. They lied.

They **really** lied!

They're not like us, honey. They've got **tails.**

"Massa had a yaller gal,
he brought her from de Souf'
Her hair it curled so very tight
She couldn't shut her mouf.

He took her to the tailor shop
To have her mouf' made small;
She swallowed up de tailor,
Tailor shop an' all."

Song from Southern USA passed down from slavery to the present.

Her soft, wide nose was
accused of taking
in too much air.
Her lips were too thick.
Her skin was too dark.
And that kinky hair...
Well....

Sun,
weather,
wind
and time
change your skin...
dry your skin ...
it's time for **envi** ...
... **envi** softness

envi makes
beautiful things happen!

"Gwine find a
beauty shop
Cause I ain't a lovely
belle.
The boys pass me by,
They say I's not so swell …
I hate that ironed hair
And dat bleaching skin …
But I'll be all alone
If I don't fall in."

Una Marson
(Jamaica/Britain)

So she reasoned that if she
looked more like Them, she'd be
treated more like Them. She
would learn to act like Them.
In fact, she decided, she
would just **be** Them.
Industries sprang up
to accomodate this.

HAIR became the first line of defense.

Hair was stretched, painted, beaten,
crimped, curled, burned, treated, lied about,
covered up and prayed over.

You too may be *Pretty!*

There's no need to worry about the hair and skin of Grace, Violet, Crystal, or your other pretty friends. Yours may be just as pretty. Use regularly—

Madam C.J. Walker's
HAIR and TOILET PREPARATIONS
"World Renowned"

Unhealthy scalps, short, dull, lifeless hair; rough, sallow, pimply skin, prevent your being pretty. They need not exist. A few regular Madam C. J. Walker treatments given by well trained Madam C. J. Walker agents using Madam C. J. Walker preparations will correct them. ¶ For long, thick, lustrous, healthy hair, nothing is better than Madam C. J. Walker's Vegetable Shampoo, Wonderful Hair Grower, Glossine, Tetter Salve. ¶ For clear, firm, smooth skin, glowing with health, you should use Madam C. J. Walker's Complexion Soap, face creams, face powders, dental cream, rouge, etc.
Stop Experimenting—
Use These Preparations Now!

50¢
Everywhere

Madam C. J. Walker's 18 Preparations for sale by Agents, Drug Stores and by Mail

The Madam C.J. Walker Mfg. Co. Inc.
640 N. West Street.
Indianapolis, Ind.

Some started borrowing
hair from other people.
Sistuhs could finally shake
their tresses in the wind.

A hair caste system emerged: "good" hair, "bad" hair, and bought hair. It caused some folks to stop eating watermelon.

circa 1910-1950

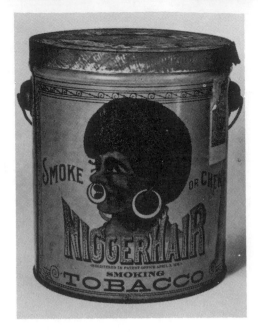

In the U.S. Black men and women are 12% of the population but buy 34% of the hair care products.

What appeared to be a physical act was really a psychological reaction.

Mothers taught baby Sistuhs to hold in their lips and pinch their noses. Hips had a hard way to go (if they went at all).

The Others' plan was in place. The BW no longer loved herself. Physically free, but mentally enslaved, for many the SPIRIT was being held hostage. Some Sistuhs got through the day by "emotionally passing for white."

But soon even Euro-centric women realized that some (more) lies had been told, and they started borrowing back the truth. ⟶

Why am I upset? I've been wearing their hair for years!

"White Women Want Fashionably Full Flappers"

"Voluptuous pouts. Cosmetic surgeons are finding ways to augment thin lips to fashionable fullness...with collagen injections...or liposuction techniques to build up the lips with transplanted fat taken from any part of the body..."

Los Angeles Times Magazine
March 26, 1989

My lips? The lips you made me hate?

My TV joke lips?!?

The ones in the racist cartoons? Les levres developpés??

...or grow your own.
Ad for padded "hips," $20.
(USA, 1992)

This triggers a run on THE BANK: Which is to say the BW gets ahold of herself and (about every 3rd generation) decides to reclaim her own Image. So she calls a press conference and declares:

"SOMEBODY ALMOST RUN OFF WITH ALLA MY STUFF!"

SHE BECOMES RIGHTEOUSLY FIRED UP—

"…stealin my shit from me/
don't make it yours/
makes it stolen/
somebody almost run off wit alla my stuff/
& i waz standin there/
lookin at myself/ the whole time/ …"

Ntozake Shange
(USA)

— FIRED UP AND DANGEROUS TO BEHOLD!

She reclaims the motherland, rituals, **black** baby dolls and praise songs.

"Homage To My Young Black Sisters" by sculptor Elizabeth Catlett (1968)

CHERYL TATUM-TANDIA, one of several women fired from their hotel jobs for wearing corn-rows. Most fought back and won.

> "May my outer head not spoil my inner head."
> Yoruba proverb

"Three-fourths of my life so far has been spent living with poverty and with shame. It's only five or six years I could actually come to love myself. As a person. As a woman. As a Black woman in particular. And now, what's so beautiful is that no one can take that away from me."

Member
National Black Women's Health Project (USA)

She reclaims her Stuff (with the right to enjoy it) and makes it hers again.

RÉPUBLIQUE GABONAISE
Coiffure authentique du Gabon
POSTES 1981
125f

"New attitudes" a hundred years apart.

And you already know what the Sistuh has, the world wants!

"*Did they bring you promises
of things to come?
Did they buy you
some beer or wine?
As the hunters devour you
with rough caresses
do they still smile and say
you are divine?*"

Archie Weller (Australia)

Madonna or Madam? The BW is worshipped as Madonna and worshipped as Whore, a dichotomy not of her own design.

The **Madonna** goes back to the earliest humans, who created their gods and goddesses based on their observations of **Nature.**

T he Holy Trinity and resurrection are in the mythology and icons of ancient Africa and Asia centuries <u>before</u> Christianity evolved.

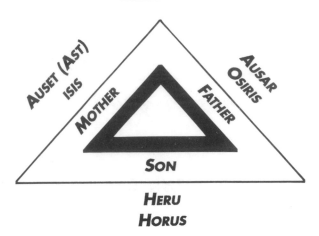

The African goddess AST or AUSET (ISIS in Greek) is the original Madonna... the mother goddess...

...the embodiment of the feminine spirit...

...the goddess of navigation and the moon.

The Madonna's power is in giving and restoring life, domestic matters, natural phenomena, initiation.

Earthenware image of Isis, from approx. 663-641 B.C.

The **Madam** developed some 4000 years ago, and blossomed in the 15th & 16th centuries A.D. as the original mythology was reshaped: Isis, acquiring the knowledge of good and evil, was divinized. The later Eve, acquiring the same knowledge, became the cause of man's fall from grace. The Bad Guy. The unclean unholy one. Banished.

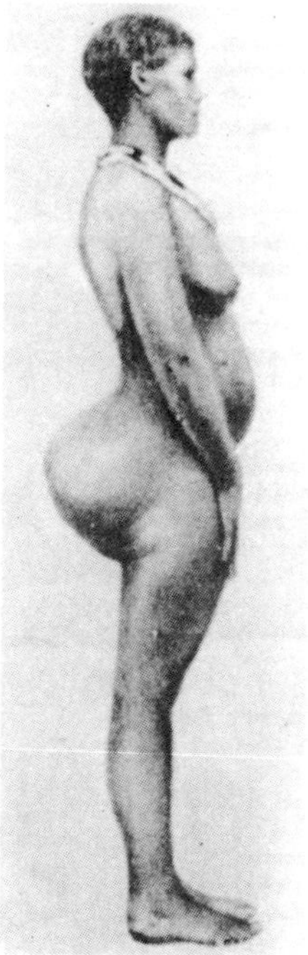

In the early 1800's Saartjie, a South African, was dubbed "The Hottentot Venus" and put on public display in London and Paris.

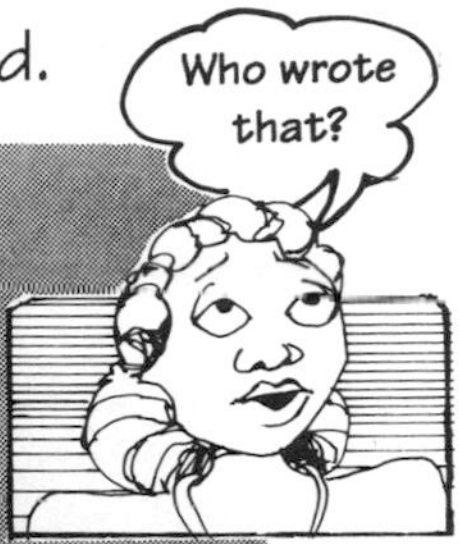
Who wrote that?

Mother/Female was dropped from the Trinity and Isis was sometimes derided as a "pagan" goddess.

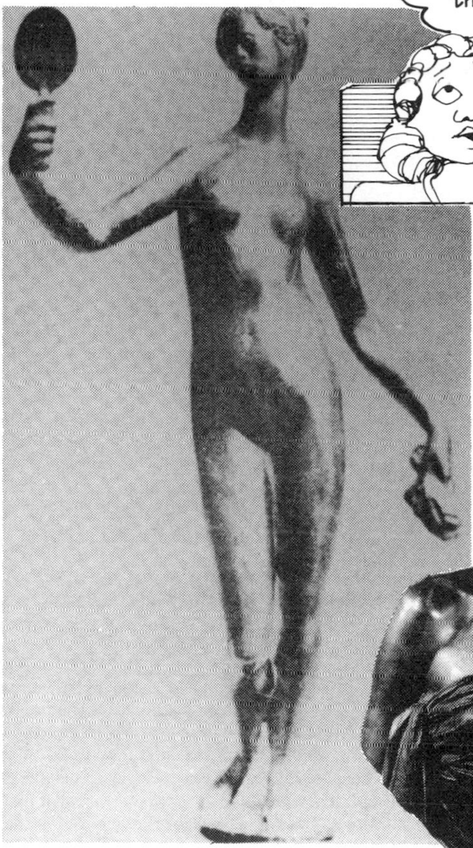

"The Black Venus," 1500's, by Italy's Allesandro Vittoria.

The BW was worshipped as the virtuous Venus. Ah, Mother love! Ah, Lust!

The Madam's power is in giving and restoring life (so to speak), domestic matters, natural phenomena, initiation.

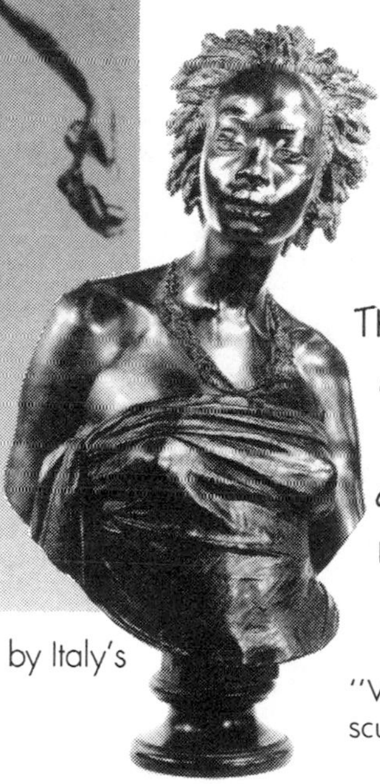

"Venus africaine" by French sculptor Charles Cordier, 1852.

In Christianity, Isis became the Virgin Mary. Naturally, she brought her bbblack and her power with her.

It was 325 years **after** the death of the prophet Jesus that the Council of Bishops of the Roman Catholic Church approved the Virgin Mary and the immaculate conception as church symbols.

"When Christians came into power after the edict of Constantine they were powerless against the great hold of the Black Madonna on the people, so they ended by compounding her religion with theirs, changing her name to Mary. It is significant that the mother of Buddha was [called] Maryamma."

J.A. Rogers,
Sex and Race (USA)

Speaking of Mary....

Jesus on gold coin, circa 705 A.D., described in a letter to W.E.B. DuBois from the collection of the Cambridge Enclyclopedia Co., London as "Jesus Christ with woolly hair...a Negro."

A uset/Isis/Black Madonna images are every-where, including some places where a **real** BW is not welcome.

Hallelujah!   Hallelujah!
Halleeeeluuujah!

POLAND RUSSIA SWITZERLAND SPAIN

There are more than 300 "Vierges Noires" just in France.

One of Europe's oldest Black Madonnas, of Loreto, Italy, was destroyed by fire in 1930 and restored by Pope Pious XI.

The Black Virgins' worshippers
include several Popes and kings.

"Pilgrims journeying to the shrine at
Mount Vergine [Italy] would climb the steps
of the church on their knees, licking each
step with their tongues. We are, thus
equating the blackness of the image
with their power."

Leonard Moss,
"In Quest Of The Black Virgin" (USA)

Those Bishop
gentlemen were
not thrilled
about the
Sistuh in their
midst and tried
to explain away
her "darkness."

"It's the
candle smoke."

"It's a spiritual
darkness."

"It's the
wood."

"It's dark
in here."

There was even a touch of Black Madonna genocide during the French Revolution and other revolts against the Church.

If **candles** caused the blackness of these figures, then why haven't candles blackened their robes, or any of the white Madonnas? Enough said. **"She is black because she is Black."**

Which seemed enough for Shakespeare, who lost his heart to "the Dark Lady of the Sonnets."

"Then will I swear beauty herself is black,
And all they foul that thy complexion lack."
Shakespeare,
Sonnet #132

Several Shakespearean scholars identify her as Lucy (Luce) Negro or Morgan, a most popular courtesan.

"The Sonnets were written around 1597 [when] London was teeming with Africans, and African women...were much courted by the young better-class men around town...African women were seen as highly desirable sex symbols...in Germany, Italy, France, Spain and Portugal."

Edward Scobie
"African Women in Early Europe"

This "chocolate fixation" was rampant in France.

The wife of King Louie XIV had a child by her African slave. The infant LOUISE-MARIE was secreted in a convent, where she gained fame as "The Black Nun of Moret."

ISABEAU was the Black diva courtesan during Louis XV's reign.

The Sudanese ISMERIA married into French royalty. Shrines were built in her honor, and after her death she was "madonna'd" as "Notre Dame de Liesse."

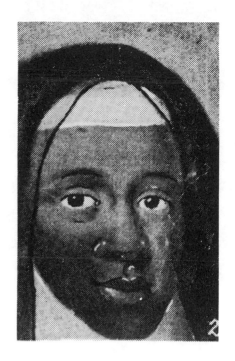

This took place while, in the Americas, sexually "having" an enslaved BW was a White male right-of-passage to manhood. She could be freely used and raped and was therefore considered—through some strange twist of perception—as wanton or amoral. The whore image prevailed on many levels.

"Next comes a warmer race, from sable sprung,
To love each thought, to lust each nerve is strung;...
These sooty dames, well vers'd in Venus' school
Make love an art, and boast they kiss by rule."

"Jamaica, A Poem, in Three Parts,"
1777 (London)

This 1908 New Orleans' **Blue Book** conveniently lists madams and prostitutes (and their services) in 🖤 categories.

Editorial cartoon on Hawaii, late 1800's

I've lyed and I've prattled <u>with</u> <u>fifty</u> <u>fair</u> <u>maids</u>
And changed them as oft d'ye see.
But of all <u>sweet</u> creatures my eyes ever saw,
A <u>Copper</u> faced damsel for me.

One of the most madonna'd madams of media brings us to

THE CLEOPATRA CONTROVERSY

"Image manipulation", or, "Beauty is in the eye of..."

Cleopatra, Queen of Egypt
Ptolemaic votive plaque

Cleopatra, Queen of Egypt
engraving by the European
J.Chapman, in 1804

Cleopatra, Queen of Egypt painting
by African-American
Earl Sweeting.

14 Cleopatra plays
3 Cleopatra films
1067 Cleopatra poems
2 operas
194 artist's renderings
11 record albums
37 T-shirts
1 coin

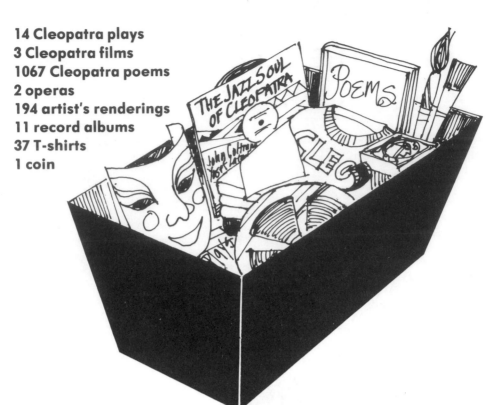

The lady's been dead for 2000 years, but folks are still fighting over her.

•

What did she have?? (And where could they get it??) She had a courtesan's style and seductiveness. She had the undivided attention of men who ruled the world, so she **made** history.

She had enemies (which makes good press)

> Obscene courtesan!

> Scheming diva!

> Whore!

She had power, and loved using it for political ends.

"I receive her as having a strong African loyalty and a political animus of high order at a time when the Greek woman was a vassal. Through her political/sexual relationships she kept the harshest aspects of the Roman Empire off of Egypt, the land she loved."

John Henrik Clarke
(USA)

There were 6 other Cleopatra's in the family before the famous one
(Theda Bara, Claudette Colbert and Liz Taylor **not** included!)

She was born in Africa in 69 B.C. and ascended the throne at age 18. By then Egypt had been conquered by, and mixed with, Assyria, Persia, Greece and Rome, and this ancient Black civilization was becoming more White. Research indicates that her mother was Persian (that's a bit African) and her father was a Greek, possibly born of an African slave woman.

Now you can do your own Cleo family tree, based on where you're coming from, remembering that the prejudices of time were of culture, not of color.

MAKEDA

—is one of the most famous Sistuhs ever! She ruled Ethiopia for 50 years when it spanned India, parts of Asia and the Mediterranean.

Makeda was a brilliant trade strategist and builder. One day she dropped by Jerusalem (with a ship full of goods and servants) to negotiate a trade agreement with King Solomon.

Bible

Koran

The Kebra Negast

a.k.a. "The Queen Of Sheba"

a.k.a. "Belkis"

"Makeda"

"I sailed West to reach East, and had to round off the earth as I went. The hair from my head thinned, and gold was made on three continents. I am so hip even my errors are correct. I am so perfect, so divine, so ethereal, so surreal I cannot be comprehended, except by my own permission..."

Nikki Giovanni (USA)

88

Solomon built her a crystal palace and a V.D. (Visiting Diva) throne. Together they created a future king, Menelik. Then Makeda took her trade agreement and stuff and sailed home. Her legendary visit is one of the world's most celebrated romances.

"My black triangle
sandwiched between the geography
     of my thighs...
My black triangle
is so rich
that it flows over
on to the dry crotch
of the world...
and though
it spares a thought
for history
my black triangle
has spread beyond his story..."

Grace Nichols (Guyana/Britain)

Frank Buchser's "Nackte Sklavin" painting, 1880, used a Moroccan model.

"I will... And all that is or ever shall be is but reverberations and repercussions of that first almighty thunderclap. I will. It is both a declaration and a command. It affirms dominion. Take a moment and whisper it to yourself. 'I will.' Feel the power."

Susan L. Taylor (USA)

Power. Since the beginning of time Black Women have wielded power, through Marriage, Matriarchal systems, the Military, and Magic.

> "**MAGIC:** (the Ancestors' definition): A management of forces, causing change to occur in conformity with will."
>
> **MAGIC:** (Others' definition): "To compel the cooperation of other people, deity or nature, in enterprises of self...known as **white magic** when ethical and as **black magic** when amoral."
>
> (Marc Edmund Jones, *Occult Philosophy*)

There they go again. Curses on them!

BWn receive, as a birthday present from their ancestors, the gift of extraordinary powers. Some call it magic. Some call it "sight." Many choose to ignore the power, others have no choice.

A Sudanese sistuh, ZAHRA, was taken to Yugoslavia in the late 1870's, where she told the future from the muscles of her right arm. She lived to be 126. Her descendants still sing of her glory today.

In what is now Zimbabwe, the incarnated medium NEHANDA used her spiritual powers to guide the Shona people in resisting British invaders.

For more than 70 years a sensuous New Orleans hairdresser, MARIE LEVEAUX, was damned for working evil (would you like to have your husband's mistress disappear?) and praised for working miracles. One writer described her as "our last great witch."

It's said that the great HARRIET TUBMAN had the gift, and used it to guide herself and other slaves to freedom.

Writer and folklorist ZORA NEALE HURSTON was one of those with the gift, but she didn't want it. As a young girl she had a vision of her entire life. It was not a pretty picture.

"I was weighted down with a power I did not want. I had knowledge before its time...I knew that I would be an orphan and homeless.. that a shotgun-built house held torture for me, but I must go. I saw a deep love betrayed but I must feel and know it. Oh, how I cried to be just as everybody else..! Time was to prove the truth of my visions, for one by one they came to pass.... It is one of the blessings of this world that few people see visions and dream dreams."

Zora Neale Hurston
Dust Tracks On A Road (USA)

ZORA NEALE HURSTON
(1903-1960) Most prolific Black
woman author of the Harlem
Renaissance

Mythology's CIRCE, "Mistress of Magic" who turns humans into hogs, on a pottery piece, 5th Cent. B.C. Of African origin, she's described by Herodotus as having black skin and woolly hair.

Since prehistoric time women and the moon—that powerful feminine entity— have had a thang.

"During the Lunar Cult period, the moon was considered the lord of women, of witches and magicians. Woman was directly connected to the moon because it regulated her menses. And because the [concept of] fatherhood was not known, the moon was seen to be the cause of her impregnation so it was through the moon that she acquired her magic."

Elaine Armour, "Woman As Goddess, Priestess, Whore" (USA)

In ancient times "magic" was not entertainment. Black communities understood the power of physical and metaphysical "protection." Magic was used to attract good and repel (or cause) evil, so a good "witch" was an asset to the community.

In the Transvaal, the RAIN QUEEN OF LOVEDU holds the secret power (and terrible responsibility) to regulate rainfall, which includes withholding it from enemies.

In some West African tribes the dead are buried only by the female elders, as it's believed they have the secret power to assist the soul on its journey between the physical and spiritual worlds.

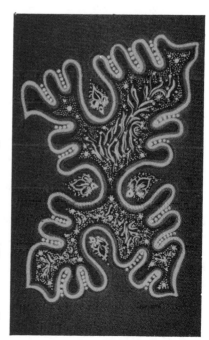

Aboriginal women use a complex system of **songs** to restore well-being to individuals or the community. They're performed while massaging the body with fat and clay. The feet are painted with designs that allow dis-ease to leave the body. Positive results are often seen within hours.

Aboriginal women's art from the
Fregon region of Australia.

Thile Magic is based on the ideas that:

1 all things of nature hold life, and can therefore be used for good or evil;

2 there's an active relationship between the living, the dead and the unborn;

3 human ability only succeeds in conjunction with spiritual power; and

4 body, mind and spirit are one (and must be dealt with accordingly.)

"Listen more often
to things than to beings;
The fire's voice is heard,
Hear the voice of the water.
It is the ancestor's breath."
Birago Diop
(Senegal)

Juju, Vodun, Ifa, Candomble, Macumba, Shamanism, incorporating these ideas, all have female priests. Their "magic" is a way of life. That's why they keep:

THE WITCH-MAGICIAN'S TOOLBOX:

The number of highest power=synthesis of body, mind, spirit. The mystery #: when multiplied it reproduces itself.

HER RESULTS:

HER RESULTS: heal your body, cure the crazies, sass up your sex life, raise social status, deter enemies, remove unwanted folks, see danger, find money (please!), increase fertility, balance fear and dispel others' curses against you.

She is witch, wisdom and warrior: mess with her and you got a problem!

To enhance psychic power make a tea of raspberry leaves. Take daily during menses.

To catch a lover, tape his picture behind your mirror.

To prevent conception brew some bloodroot bark, add red pepper and a teaspoon of gunpowder. Drink a little at each new moon.

"She knew wonderful simples for ailments of body and soul, and bound up both in earthy ointments. We…hung asafetida bags around our necks when there were epidemics in town, ate sulphur and cream of tartar each spring, stayed away from graveyards after dark as she taught us to do,… and following her precepts we prospered as did her own children."

Lillian Smith
Killers Of The Dream, 1949 (USA)

"Don't look for her power
in the eyes,
or the thighs,
Look in her hair
There are secrets birthing there."

The BW has an exclusive on some works. Her power is in the sacred secretness of her knowledge. It's called:

THE BLACK WOMAN'S SECRETS: ▶

(That's why she calls them secrets.)

There's always somebody standing around feeling threatened by this sort of power (naturally.)

In the Colonies in 1692 a slave from Barbados, TITUBA INDIAN, was among the first women tried in the famous Salem (Mass.) Witchcraft Trials.

She was guilty of being too good with her hands as a weaver and healer. Condemned to hang at age 32, Tituba was later pardoned, then purchased out of slavery.

Fanatical early Christians tried to suppress free thinking by attacking and butchering HYPATIA, a young Egyptian philosophy teacher.

In the colonial settlements of Northern Australia, native women practicing the complex social/religious rituals that manage emotions have been accused by European missionaries of being witches, practicing "love magic."

During the 16th and 17th centuries several million women were destroyed in Europe and America, for being involved in the healing arts. (Some folks would just rather wait for god Herself.)

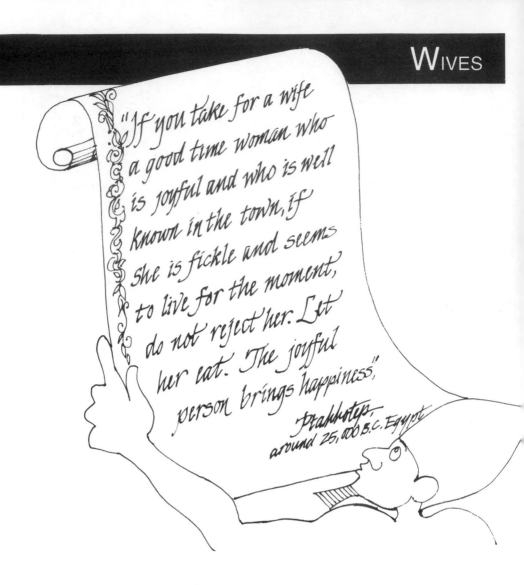

"If you take for a wife a good time woman who is joyful and who is well known in the town, if she is fickle and seems to live for the moment, do not reject her. Let her eat. The joyful person brings happiness."

Ptahhotep, around 25,000 B.C. Egypt

WIVES are sometimes mistaken for—in the lesser sense of the word— witches.

Even when they're not (witches), Black wives are likely to show up where you least expect them.

The early royalty of Hawaii were Polynesians on the Black side of the family. KA'AHUMANU, "favorite wife" of Kamehameha the Great, initiated an end to the "kapu" system of taboos that segregated men from women in many social acts, including meals.

Hawaii's Queen Ka'ahumanu
(1768-1832)

In China,

"The ancient Tartars were an aboriginal... blackskinned people...Tartar women were not only equal with their men, but fought alongside them.... Among ancient Chinese, it was the privilege for men to have as their great wife a Tartar."

James Brunson
"African Presence In Early China" (USA)

The 7th Vice-President of the United States, Richard Johnson, almost lost the nomination because of his husbandly relationship with a Sistuh, JULIA CHINN, who gave him two daughters.

"Although many white southern politicians kept black concubines and sired mulatto offspring...each could display a white wife and a brood of legitimate children... Johnson was not being taken to task for his liaison with a woman of color; rather, he was being-persecuted for his 'scorn of secrecy.'"

Catherine Clinton,
The Plantation Mistress (USA)

"I love my master but every night
When I cross the blossoming path to the
    canefield
the secret place of our acts of love,
I see myself knife in hand,
flaying him like an innocent animal.
Bewitching drumbeats
now drown his cries, his sufferings,
The bells of the sugar-mill call..."

Nancy Morejon (Cuba)

103

When Sistuh-wives have had
complete freedom, they've made a
mark on world history.

"The most important of the Ethiopian Queens
were independent rulers: their husbands were consorts
to them. These queens [1000 B.C. - 1000 A.D.] ran
the civil administration, led armies against military foes,
promoted long-distance commerce and diplomatic
relations, and engaged in massive building programs.
In every way, they exercised the full
prerogatives and powers of rulership."

Larry Williams, Charles S. Finch,
"The Great Queens of Ethiopia" (USA)

Ethiopian QUEEN AMENIRDAS, 25th Dynasty, late 8th Century B.C.

Consort: spouse or partner of a reigning king or queen.

AMY JACQUES GARVEY, 2nd wife of Black nationalist Marcus Garvey. Editing and publishing her late husband's writings has helped keep his legacy and teachings alive.

NELSON and WINNIE MANDELA. She carried on his work against South Africa's apartheid system while he was imprisoned for 28 years, and she was imprisoned intermittently. They had only two full years together during their first 32 years of marriage.

"I am a living symbol of the white man's fear."

Winnie Mandela,
Part Of My Soul Went With Him
(South Africa)

political activist JOSINA MACHEL

Josina and Samora Machel met when both were leaders in Mozambique's armed struggle against the Portuguese, and married in 1969. He became independent Mozambique's first President. Her death, April 7th, is still marked yearly as National Women's Day.

105

3 of history's most fascinating wives are AHMOSE-NEFERTERE, TIYE and her daughter-in-law NEFERTITI, all queens of Egypt's 18thDynasty.

Do not confuse sistuhs
Nefertere,
Nefertari, &
Nefertiti

AHMOSE-NEFERTERE, wife of Ahmose, helped rebuild Egypt after they drove out invaders. She was the first "Divine Wife," and therefore considered equal to the gods.

The Nubian beauty TIYE was 13 when she entered an "arranged" political marriage with Egyptian Pharoah Amenhotep III.

"The most praised, the lady of grace,
Sweet in her love, who fills the palace with her beauties..."

Amenhotep and the Miracles

TIYE reined for 50 years, giving birth to Egypt's famous sons, Akhenaten and King Tutenkhamen. She had her own library, strongly influenced her husband, and handled foreign affairs after he died. Most believe her relationship saved the Nubians from total submission to Egypt.

Funerary sculpture for the royal couple. Tiye's size in the sculpture, relative to Amenhotep's, indicates her equal status.

NEFERTITI and her husband Akhenaten (Amenhotep IV) created six daughters and introduced stunning changes in Egyptian religion and culture. He built monuments in her honor. After his death Nefertiti fought rebellious priests to maintain her husband's reforms.

NEFERTITI AND AKHENATEN, 1300's B.C.

Power was also gained through kinship systems which traced the rights of secession through a female. Kinship is the foundation of MATRIARCHY.

In recent years MATRIARCHY has become a naughty word!

The bad press got worse when sociologist Daniel Moynihan issued his 1965 government report, "The Negro Family: The Case For National Action," which is still being used against the BW.

The Modern Matriarch Myth

It alleges that Black women have political and social power over their lives and use it to emasculate Black men (when in fact Black men and women both live primarily under decisions made by White males), and part of the solution was to make the Black man king of the castle—read: patriarchy.

Sistuhs responded! The White middle class patri-
archal "norm," they said, had already proved itself

Therefore: Let the record show that:

1. Matriarchy has existed for at least 7000 years.
2. Neither anti-male nor pro-female, it is a system of organization that allows for orderly secession of power and continuity
within the community.
3. The original matriarchal systems provided women with certain social and economic security.

So. . . WHAT'S WRONG WITH BEING A MATRIARCH??

NOTHING!

In some societies, such as South Africa's Lovedu tribe, the female ruler and wealthy women marry a "wife." This complicated social structure is based mostly on the property transfer of cattle, and provides the female "husband" with extra help.

"Everything that touches your life must be an instrument of your liberation, or you must throw it into the trash can of history."
John Henrik Clarke (USA)

BWn have a heavy warrior tradition.

Greece and Rome took control of Egypt, then went after Cush (ancient Ethiopia.) AMANIRENAS, one of five Black "Candace Queens," responded by attacking their Egyptian cities. Augustus Caesar withdrew, possibly because Amanirenas controlled much of Africa's trade in luxury goods.

QUEEN KAHINA, a Hebrew, resisted the new Islam religion in the 7th century. In what is now Tunisia, her armies forced the Arabs to retreat. But, divining that her people would eventually fall under Arab rule, she scorched the earth so the conquerers would not prosper from it.

One sistuh didn't wait to be attacked. The Ethiopian QUEEN JUDITH, a Falasha Jew (still Black) and military leader, was death on Christianity and **initiated** a war against it. She **won** and ruled Abyssinia for 40 years.

Being a warrior woman was not without sacrifice! Legend has it that Dahomey's female archers, bodyguards to King Benhanzin, cut off their right breast (serious sacrifice!) in order to increase their shooting skill.

All these sistuhs performed **before** Joan of Arc, whom White historians often hold up as "the first notable she-soldier."

A Tassili (Algeria) wall painting made thousands of years ago. Some archeologists think she is a precursor to Dahomey's warrior women archers.

The difference between women-who-go-to-war and **women warriors** is that the 2nd group is usually leading a **liberation** stuggle. The period of modern colonialism, 1400's to 2000, could be titled, on the field of life,

THE BLACK
QUEENS
vs.
THE WHITE
SUPREMES

QUEENS
VS
SUPREMES

What was the prize?.

Land, mineral resources and human labor.

NZINGHA, NEHANDA, SARROUNIA, KAIPKIRE
YAA ASANTEWA, NANNY, WALLOA, ZEFERINA

PORTUGAL, BRITAIN, GERMANY, FRANCE BELGIUM

NEHANDA, Zimbabwe,
vs. British, 1890's

YAA ASANTEWA, Gold Coast (Ghana)
vs. British, 1900 ▶

KAIPKIRE & Herero Women, Namibia,
vs. Germans, 1904-1906

SARROUNIA, Niger,
vs. French, early 1900's

the WOMEN'S ARMY of Dahomey,
vs. French, 1890's ▼

Ashanti Queen Mother
YAA ASANTEWA in 1900 led her
people against the British, the last
battle of a 100 year war.

At age 60 Angola's QUEEN NZINGHA
(aka Jinga) was still leading her warriors
into battle against the Portuguese, dressed
in men's clothing and preferring to be called
"king." She strategized successfully against
the Portuguese, and when her brother made
a pact with them against his own people,
she had him killed. ▼

NZINGHA, Angola, vs.
Portugese, 1800's

114

Hidden in these warrior stories are some unkind acts—poisonings, disposition of family traitors, etc.—performed by Sistuhs to meet the bottom line: freedom from European domination.

"The rebel woman, who with pin
pricked the soft mold of
her own child's head
sending the little newborn soul
winging its way back to Africa,
<u>free!</u>"
Grace Nichols (Guyana)

These are just the daintier acts of war. (The rest is on the evening news.)

As colonialism and slavery spread, more BWn led liberation movements:

"Now you have
touched the
women
you have struck a rock
You have dislodged a
boulder
You will be crushed."

South African women's anti-passbook campaign song, 1956

•SPAIN   •GERMANY
•BRITIAN   •FRANCE
•UNITED STATES •PORTUGAL
•BELGIUM   •NETHERLANDS

QUEENS vs. SUPREMES

•ANNA de BENGAL, Mauritius, vs. Dutch, 1600's
•NANNY, Jamaica, vs. Spanish, 1600's
•MAMA PANSA, Surinam, vs. Dutch, 1800's
•WALLOA, Tasmania, vs. British, 1830
•HARRIET TUBMAN, United States, vs United States, 1800's
•LYDIA LILI'UOKALANI, Hawaii, vs. USA, late 1800's
•ANNE HELGARD, Virgin Islands, vs. Denmark, 1840's
•ZEFERINA, Brazil, vs. Portuguese, 1826

Lydia Lili 'Uokalani

In 1830 the Tasmanian Sistuh WALLOA led a five-day uprising against the internment of her tribe. Under British imperialism Tasmanian women were raped, stolen, forced into hard labor in the whaling industry and had their children taken from them. Their strongest weapon became refusing to procreate within the tribe.

"There was one of two things I had a right to, liberty or death. If I could not have one I should have the other, for no man should take me alive."

HARRIET ROSS TUBMAN, (1823-1913, USA) pulled a gun on her own husband during a slave escape. After leading hundreds of slaves to freedom she became a spy for the Union Army, and is said to be the only woman, Black or White, to successfully execute a military campaign behind enemy lines.

Hundreds of captured Africans brought to Surinam escaped into the interior bush. Oral histories praise MAMA PANSA, who braided rice seeds in her hair before escaping so her people could plant them and survive.

Brazil's ZEFERINA, head of a community of Yoruba slave fugitives near Bahia, organized a revolt against plantation masters in 1826.

Legends say NANNY OF THE MAROONS was so powerful she could "stop bullets with her buttocks." A town in Jamaica is named for her.

Today, while some of the sisterhood battles for "upward mobility" (tenure / travel / and a good manicurist) the other half is fighting for breath itself.

Fighting:

AGAINST **Imperialism**

(imperialism:)
domination of economic & political affairs
control of raw materials
military aggression
dissemination of disease
creation of refugees through war and land
  claims
spread of misinformation
control of family life (and private parts)
decimation of the male population

FOR **Freedom**

(freedom:)
a roof, a meal, dignity, help
health care
nourished, educated children
freedom from economic stress
self-determination

SWAPO women commanders in the field during Namibia's revolutionary struggle against South Africa.

Their front line has real bullets.

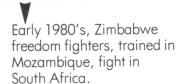

Early 1980's, Zimbabwe freedom fighters, trained in Mozambique, fight in South Africa.

These Sistuh-soldiers can't leave their woman thang at home. Without adequate supplies, they often use grass and leaves during their menses. Some choose modern birth control over tribal tradition in order to stay active in the war. Others leave their newborns in a liberation army nursery (creche) and return to the front lines. Their objective is freedom first.

photo: Ron Wilkins

A Sandanista BW at Pearl Lagoon, Nicaragua, 1984.

"I have not come to tell you you are lovely. That you are beautiful I do believe but that is not what it is all about. The matter is they wish that you were dead."

Nicolas Guillen (Cuba), to Angela Davis

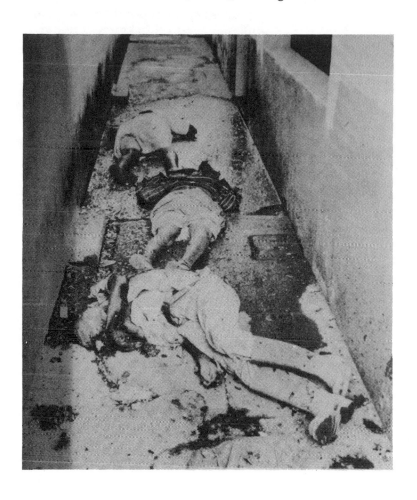

Sharpesville, 1969: 76 persons dead, 20,000 detained

**"when you have emptied our calabashes
into your porcelain bowls overflowing**

Soweto, 1976: 700 persons dead

**the surplus spilling and seeping
into foreign soil**

Birmingham, 1963: 4 Black girls dead

**when you have cleaved the heads of our young
and engraved upon the soft papyrus there**

Grenada, 1983: 200+ persons dead

an erasure of our past. . .
. . .

Panama, 1989: 21 mental patients bombed

"The Rhodesians bombed the whole camp...the largest number who died were schoolchildren...800 comrades died in that place...We had our medical center there and most of the patients died..."

Nyasha , describing 1977 attack on Chimoi, a Mozambique base. (Zimbabwe)

**We will rebuild
we will choose our most knowing
most eloquent old women
to spit in the mouths
of the newborn babies
so that they will remember
. . .
so that if you come again
in another time
with your trinkets and arms
with porcelain bowls
and scriptures
they will say
we know you."**

Iyamide Hazeley (Britain)

122

"I'll tell you why I did all these things. It is very simple. I did all these things because they needed to be done."

Marie Grace Augustin, planter
(St. Lucia)

123

A warrior queen who would not war is HATSHEPSUT, ruler of Egypt's 18th Dynasty for 30 some years. Her strengths were rebuilding, massive trade expeditions and aggressive leadership. She **took** the throne from its male heir and declared herself Pharoah, even dressing as a male.

Hatshepsut, Egypt's 18th Dynasty 1505-1485 B.C., considered the greatest female leader of all time.

We dub her the patron ancestor of the MOVERS & SHAKERS.

(monument inscription:)

"I have restored that which is in ruins, I have raised up that which was unfinished."

Over the last 300 years the Movers &
Shakers have punched a heavy time
clock, doing double time,
overtime and jail time.

Why movements??

The Problem: **Racism** and
Sexism (which means one
movement can't be
separated from another)
The Price: **Body** and **Spirit**
The Prize: **Self-determination** and a
protected freedom

ABOLITION

After three centuries of chattel slavery world-wide, the movement to abolish it finally took hold. ABOLITION was the major movement of the 19th century.

Despite his/story giving most of the credit to Whites, Black abolitionists carried equal weight and BWn were popular abolition speakers throughout the Americas and Europe.

MARIA STEWART'S 1832 anti-slavery speech in Boston was considered audacious, as women of that time weren't supposed to speak in public.

In 1851 ELIZA PARKER was among those arrested for resisting a slaveowner's attempt to reclaim his escaped slaves under the Fugitive Slave Act. The slaveowner was killed and Eliza was put on trial twice before escaping to Canada.

SARAH MAPPS DOUGLASS, a devout Quaker, and her mother helped found the Philadelphia Female Anti-Slavery Society. The Quakers supported abolition but kept Sarah in segregated seating at their meetings.

In the Virgin Islands, legends credit
ANNE HELGAARD (1790-1859) with bringing slavery to a halt
through her intimate relationship with the Danish Governor.

The gap between the end of the slave trade and the end of <u>real</u> slavery was, in some countries, as long as 60 years. Several years after Emancipation slaves from the U.S.A. were still being smuggled into Cuba.

EDUCATION

Africans built the world's first libraries and universities.

"**A** race now rejected for their sable skin and frizzled hair founded... those civil and religious systems, arts and sciences, which still govern the universe..."

Count Constantin de Volney, *Voyage en Egypie et Syrie* (1787) and *Ruins; Revolution of Empires* (France)

Blacks knew that education was something worth having 'cause their oppressors tried to keep it from them.

Even whites were jailed for the "crime" of teaching slaves.

"Startin' now, it's against the law for y'all to vote, read, go to school, be unemployed or get too friendly with White folks."

SPELLI

CONTANCE BAKER MOTLEY was part of the NAACP's legal team that won the landmark 1954 U.S. Supreme Court decision outlawing racially segregated schools. She was the first Black American woman to become a Federal judge.

11,000 U.S. government troops were sent to protect 9 Black children who integrated a White school in 1957.

SOUTH AFRICA

In North America, MARY JANE MCLEOD BETHUNE (1875-1955) symbolizes the "education-is-the-key" philosophy. With $1.50 she opened a small school in Florida and nurtured it into the prestigious Bethune-Cookman College. Today it boasts some 10,000 alumni.

Bethune's bronze statue, Washington, D.C.

"Thirst for education. Knowledge is the prime need of the hour."

Bethune became an advisor on "Negro issues" to U.S. Presidents, and was part of the body that formed the United Nations.

Bethune's contemporary, ANNA JULIA COOPER (1858-1964), taught school for 45 years, received her doctorate from Paris' reknowned Sorbonne Univ. at the age of 66, then opened a university in her home so working Blacks could attend college at night. She lived to be 105.

Even with this kind of talent on the planet, it took more than 100 years for Spelman College, one of the world's most prestigious schools for Black Women, to put a Black woman at its helm.

DR. JOHNETTA COLE, anthropologist, author and educator, in 1987 became President of Spelman College.

Movers & Shakers face educational systems that ignore the BWn's survival needs—

"Wives of former Portuguese officials infiltrated our organization and became 'responsibles.' [Our] women were learning how to cook desserts with eggs when they had no eggs at home or to crochet doilies for tables when they had no tables."

Anabella Rodrigues,
Organization of Mozambican Women, 1979

—and leave the women
to create systems that work:

"112 over 75...
equals??"

In South Africa's
Natal Province a
hospital director
provides arithmetic
and English
classes with
health care.

Mothers build their own creche
(nursery) where they then learn
sewing, literacy and the politics of
male virility.

Gabon 1966 literacy campaign

In Jamaica, AMY BAILEY wanted to give dignity to domestics.
She opened the Homecraft Training Center in 1942 so
Jamaican women could learn "cooking, catering, morality and
mannerisms." Six thousand women had graduated by the mid
1970's.

Liberation movements created their own curriculums:

SUFFRAGE & REPRESENTATION

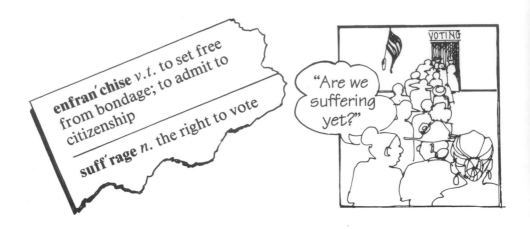

enfran'chise *v.t.* to set free from bondage; to admit to citizenship

suff'rage *n.* the right to vote

"Are we suffering yet?"

VOTING

The power of the vote is crucial to real self-determination.

In South Africa, where Black men and women have not been allowed self-determination for more than 300 years, voting is described as "something that White people do."

In Mozambique and New Guinea women didn't win the right to vote until 1975.

Women's suffrage was won in the U.S. in 1920, and in Great Britain in 1928. But not for **all** women...

While White women fought to obtain voting rights for the members of their **sex,** BWn fought to obtain the vote for their **people,** and hoped that as women they would be included.

When they were <u>excluded</u>, BWn continued the battle to win suffrage for **women,** certain that they would be included.

"We prefer Bridget and Dinah at the ballot box to Patrick and Sambo!"

Elizabeth Cady Stanton

Uh-oh!

The Alpha Suffrage Club, the first group of Black women suffragists in the United States, was organized in Chicago by journalist IDA B. WELLS-BARNETT in 1913.

40 years later many Blacks were still denied the vote through so-called literacy tests, real estate requirements, job loss and outright physical terror.

FANNIE LOU HAMER, a Mississippi, U.S.A. sharecropper with a 6th grade education, almost lost her life during years of struggle for Black voter registration. She survived and helped unseat an all-White delegation at the 1968 Democratic Convention.

ENFRANCHISEMENT ▶ REPRESENTATION ▶ POWER TO CHANGE
(VOTE)

*O*nce enfranchised, BWn moved on the political system with a mission.

DIANE ABBOTT, in 1987 became the first BW elected to Britain's Parliament in its 700 year history.

MARTA GABRE-TSADICK was the first woman Senator of Ethiopia, under Emperor Haile Selassie.

PRINCESS ELIZABETH NYABONGO, a fashion model, served as Uganda's Minister of Foreign Affairs and an Ambassador under Idi Amin.

ROSEMARY BROWN, a Jamaican, was the first BW to hold office in any Canadian Parliament. Elected to the Legislature of British Columbia in 1972, she was reelected three times.

BENEDITA da SILVA, Brazilian Congresswoman, helped structure the new Brazilian Constitution adopted in 1988 in response to Blacks' demands for equality.

"My role is more that of a catalyst. By...trying to strip off the masks that make people comfortable in the midst of chaos, perhaps I can help get things moving."

Shirley Chisholm,
Unbought and Unbossed
(USA)

SHIRLEY CHISHOLM, a former nursery schoolteacher, was the first Black U.S. Congresswoman and, in 1972, the first Black and first woman to seek the Presidency with a major political party.

WELFARE

Welfare in the original sense means to **fare well**, in one's health, prosperity, and state of mind.

The welfare of a community begins with the well fare of its women.

There is a direct correlation between well faring women and their:

1) access to natural resources

2) education level

3) life expectancy rate

In Sierra Leone in 1985, only nine percent of the women were literate, and their life expectancy was only 33 1/2 years.

"Today is the birthday of my daughter, Vera Eunice. I can't give her a party for this would be like trying to grab ahold of the sun with my hands.... Today there is nothing to eat. I wanted to invite the children for a mutual suicide, but I resisted."

Carolina Maria deJesus,
Child Of The Dark (Brazil)

Carolina Maria de Jesus

Women who do not fare well:

- add sawdust to food to make it seem like more
- are paid half of what men earn for the same work
- have no money for health care
- endure economic and sexual exploitation in the government centers designed to help them
- are most susceptible to mental disorders
- put most of their energy into food gathering
- feed their children before themselves, and
- are most likely to die from starvation.

More than one-half of the BWn in the "civilized" world do not fare well.

**"There oughta be a woman can break
Down, sit down, break down, sit
down
Like everybody else call it quits..."**

Help comes from pooling resources, education and organizing. Nigeria's First Lady, MARYAM BABANGIDA, founded the Better Life Programme (BLP) in 1987 to empower rural women. They formed health centers, over 12,000 cooperatives, and at-home businesses that have produced consumer products and significantly increased food production.

Maryam Babangida

TASO, one of Africa's first self-help groups for those with the AIDS virus, was started in Uganda in 1986 by NOREEN KALEEBA.

**"...biting her lips and lowering her eyes
To make sure there's food on the table
And wouldn't she be surprised
If the world was as willing as she's able..."**

JANE EDNA HUNTER started the Working Girls Home Assoc. in Ohio in 1911, to provide respectable housing for single BWn entering the labor force. Condemned by some for "hindering integration," her efforts grew into the Phyllis Wheatley Association, which still provides low-cost housing and social centers for "ladies of color" in many large cities.

**"...A way outa no way is flesh outa flesh
Courage that cries out at night..."**

MUM SHIRL is a legend in Australia, using her own resources to administer to Aboriginal prisoners and their families, until "the system" became too sophisticated to welcome her grass roots services.

**"...A way outa no way is flesh outa flesh
Bravery that's kept outa sight..."**

In Surinam, SOPHIE REDMOND, the country's first BW medical doctor, wrote theatrical plays to raise the consciousness of women and children.

**"...A way outa no way is too much to ask,
Too much of a task
For any one woman."**

**June Jordan
(USA)**

LABOR

Women demonstrate with the South African Congress of Trade Unions

Women co-founded two of Trinidad's major labor unions which still exist today.

MASS MEETING

TO-NIGHT

THURSDAY 7TH JULY 1938, AT 7.30 P.M. SHARP

at 66 George Street

Renewal of Protest Shop Hours Ordinance Bill.

THE WORKING CLASSES OF ALL COUNTRIES PROTEST AGAINST ANY ATTACK THAT TENDS TO REDUCE THEIR LIVING STANDARD TO ONE OF MISERY, STARVATION, AND DEATH.

THE RECENT SHOP HOURS BILL THAT HAS BEEN PASSED BY THE LEGISLATIVE COUNCIL, IF PUT INTO EFFECT WILL BRING IN ITS TRAIN INTOLERABLE HARDSHIP ON THE TOILING MASSES OF THIS COUNTRY.

The Pretended Pretext of this Bill, if such Talk of Protecting the Clerk is True

Come TO-NIGHT and Hear FRANCOIS, PERCIVAL, and PAYNE.

Outstanding Negro Leaders.—The N. W. Cul. & Social Assoc.

SUPPORT THE NEGRO WELFARE CULTURAL AND SOCIAL ASSOCIATION

For Better Living Conditions

JOIN NOW

144

CIVIL RIGHTS

The Civil Rights struggle is an old one
that keeps repeating.

ROSA PARKS' refusal, in 1955, to give up her bus seat to a White person in Alabama sparked a movement.

In 1877 IDA B. WELLS sued the State of Tennessee for segregated train seating, but lost.

MARY ELLEN "MAMMY" PLEASANT successfully sued the City of San Francisco in the 1860's for forcibly removing her from a streetcar, thus ending the ban against Black riders.

LILLIAN NGOYI was charged with high treason for leading her South African sistuhs in one of the country's biggest protests against women carrying "passbooks." Most of the last 18 years of her life were spent under house arrest.

ALBERTINA SISSULU, co-leader of South Africa's aggressive United Democratic Front and mother of seven, has spent nearly twenty years confined to her house under government "banning orders."

And repeating.

In 1938 ELMA FRANÇOISE, a laundress and labor leader in Trinidad/Tobago, was tried "for uttering words having a seditious intention." She handled her own defense and was acquitted in three days.

IDA B. WELLS' book documented lynchings in the U.S. over a 30-year period after Emancipation. The BWn's Club Movement grew out of her anti-lynching crusade.

PRICE 25 CENTS

A RED RECORD.

Tabulated Statistics and Alleged Causes of

Lynchings In the United States,

1892-1893-1894.

Respectfully submitted to the Nineteenth Century civilization in "the Land of the Free and the Home of the Brave."

BY
MISS IDA B. WELLS.
128 Clark Street,
CHICAGO.

A century later, in 1981, BEULAH MAE DONALD's 19-year-old son was lynched in Alabama. Donald tracked down the killers herself, and won a financial judgement against them.

Within each of the struggles has been a second battleground: denied equal rights with her own men.

"What is wrong in woman's life
In man's cannot be right."
Frances E.W. Harper (1895) (USA)

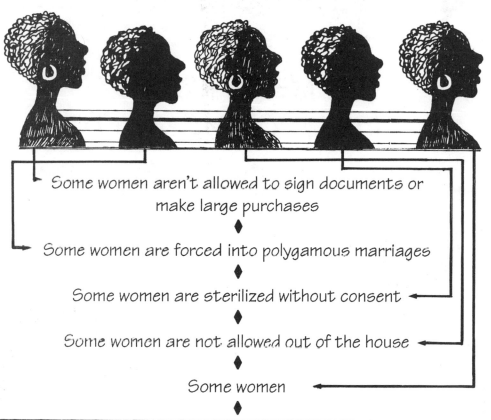

Some women aren't allowed to sign documents or make large purchases

♦

Some women are forced into polygamous marriages

♦

Some women are sterilized without consent

♦

Some women are not allowed out of the house

♦

Some women

♦

"Most men still don't have the faintest idea what our struggle is about. [It] isn't just to…go into bars, or have two or three husbands, as some men have [several wives]. We're fighting to have equal power in the management of affairs. At the moment we have an equal vote but we don't have an equal voice."

Orquidea Saraiva, 1987 (Angola)

"...
sometimes
as women only
do we weep
we are taught to whisper
when we wish to scream
assent

when we wish to defy
dance pretty
   (on tiptoe)
when we would raise circles of
dust
before the charge."

Gloria Gayles
(USA)

Which is why there has had to be a:

WOMEN'S RIGHTS/ LIBERATION MOVEMENT

But in a movement designed to eliminate restrictions **on** women, restrictions have fallen **between** women.

Like, "Women" being used in sociological writings to assume only "White Anglo-Saxon women"... as in the often used-term "Women and Blacks."

Racism has been the thorn between White and Black women seeking the same political results.

"White women were also active as abolitionists, but their failure to work with more than a token number of Black women foretold the conflicts that would later arise in the woman's rights movement...Black women were absent from the first major feminist convention at Seneca Falls, New York, in 1848..."

Jean Carey Bond,
"From the Bottom Up"
(USA)

148

It never hurts to have some **back-up,** so
Movers & Shakers did a lot of work through:

THE CLUB MOVEMENT

Their mission was to challenge racism, protect
the sisterhood and elevate the race.

1800's — Brazil: Boa Morte, originally an anti-slavery society,
is one of the oldest BWn's organi-
zations in the western hemisphere
and still exists.

1832 — USA: Afric-American Female
Intelligence Society of Boston (a
literary circle) sponsored one of
the first BWn abolitionist
speakers.

1896 — USA: Nat'l Assoc. of Colored
Women, a merger of clubs founded earlier by Mary Church
Terrell and Josephine Ruffin, focused on race issues.
Their motto:
"Lift As We Climb."

1902 — Canada: Coloured Women's Club of Montreal evolved
from a support group for Boer War victims.

1905 — USA: League For The Protection of Colored Women,
which merged to become the Nat'l Urban League.

1935 — Trinidad and Tobago: Negro Welfare Cultural and Social
Association which created the first labor unions for the
government, trade, sailors and waterfront workers.

1935 — USA: Nat'l Council of Negro Women founded by Mary McLeod Bethune as an umbrella for the many BWn's clubs, with a focus on Black economic power.

As her voice grew stronger, the "club" evolved, priorities intensified.

1945 — Mozambique: Women's Wing of FRELIMO, organized by Josina Machel, engaged in armed combat to win independence.

1950 — Brazil: Nat'l Council of Black Women, founded by Maria Nascimento.

1954 — South Africa: Federation of South African Women, Lillian Ngoyi was its President for 22 years.

1963 — Angola: Organizacao da Muher Angolana mobilized support for the independence movement. Since independence it has worked for women's education, working conditions and political participation.

1967 — Ethiopia: General Union of Eritrean Women formed in Cairo.

1970 — Women's Council of SWAPO (South West African People's Org.), to enable women to participate in the armed struggle for independence.

1983 — USA: Black Women's Health Network, focuses on improving the health status of women and their communites.

NATIONAL BLACK WOMEN'S HEALTH PROJECT

"Struggle is the friction that holds Black people together."

Septima Clarke (USA)

Now, if the truth be told...

...some Sistuhs moved and shaked to a spastic drummer, and became part of the **problem** instead of the **solution:**

The Tasmanian Trugannini assisted in the rounding up of her people, thinking they would be better off on the reserves. It led to their extinction.

In the early 1800's several free and wealthy Black women in Virginia owned slaves.

As an FBI (U.S. Federal Bureau of Investigation) undercover agent, JULIA BROWN snitched on Black folks during the outrageous anti-Communist "witch-hunts" of the 1950's. She was praised by the U.S. Congress for her work.

EMILY WEST, known as "The Yellow Rose of Texas."

I know that song. Black folks wrote that song.

'She's the sweetest rose of color
A fellow ever knew
Her eyes are bright as diamonds,
They—

Hush! Ms. West, through a romantic liason, helped the U.S. take the area now called Texas away from Mexico. Another case of the U.S.A. snatching land that didn't belong to them.

Well hush my mouth!

We already did.

The original make-it-happen, get-it-done divas are, of course, **MOTHERS.** They do **not** come by this skill naturally. They get it by going to The Black Mothers School. (a requirement).

"The Race cheer:"
"You can do anything that any other kind can do!"

"Economic policy:"
"The Lord helps them who help themselves!"

"The Law of Gravity:"
"Girl, keep your head up and your skirt down."

"The Isis Creed:"
"I brought you into this world and I will take you out of it!"

Generations of Black mothers did double duty: mothering another race and their own at the same time.

The Movers & Shakers are neither larger than life nor other than **us**. They were/are everyday women who became special by responding to their people's needs.

"International Year Of The Woman" stamp, 1975 (Burkina Faso)

"what about
full moons and sojourner
slow music
and harriet
what about those
nights in the heat
when they didn't
have to run or hide
or pray
no speech or plea
to convince anyone
of their power
those nights
when they laid there
naked, alone or with
        another
clean sheets, one small
        candle
flowers in a glass
the slow easy rise
of their stomachs
the slow, easy spread
of their breast."

Safiya Henderson Holmes,
(USA)

``Corn girl
workin for de devil
Corn girl
taking dictation like a bumble-bee
yea you make music on typewriter
yea you make carbon copies sing

. . .

you make work seem like
    a bugalu, now
Corn girl. . .''

Ras Poet Ojenke, (USA)

Takin' Care of Business
... also known as **T.C.B.**"

T.C.B. means keeping your hands on some $ $ $.
And the BW has always known
how to do that.

This phenomena is called:
THE BW AND THE
BIG

Azie Taylor **M**orton

Maggie Walker

Queen **M**akeda

Mammy Pleasant

Biddy **M**ason

Madame Tinubu

May Mason

Madame C. J. Walker

AZIE TAYLOR MORTON
was the 36th Treasurer
of the United States,
(1977-81) under
Pres. Jimmy Carter.

Sculptor SELMA BURKE designed the
Franklin D. Roosevelt dime in 1943.

Dahomey Monetary Stamp, 1972

The "Dinah" bank made in England, 1911. The eyes roll when a coin is placed in the mouth.

MAY B. MASON staked a gold claim in the Yukon mining territory in 1898, finding gold dust valued (back then) at $5,000.

Trinidadian DOUNNE MOORE heated up England with her bottled bar-b-que sauce, winning honors as a top business woman.

159

There are monuments in Nigeria to
MADAME TINUBU (IYALODE). In the early 1800's she
gained wealth as a middleman in slavery, later
trading in war supplies.

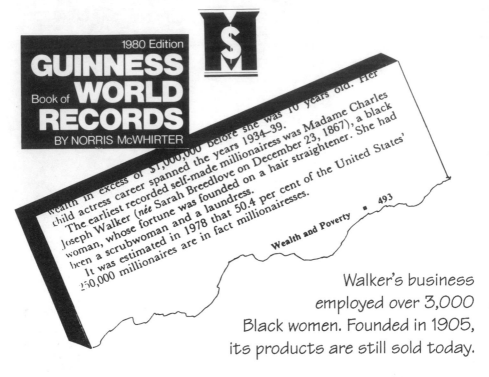

1980 Edition

GUINNESS
Book of **WORLD**
RECORDS
BY NORRIS McWHIRTER

wealth in excess of $1,000,000 before she was 10 years old. Her
child actress career spanned the years 1934–39.
The earliest recorded self-made millionairess was Madame Charles
Joseph Walker (*née* Sarah Breedlove on December 23, 1867), a black
woman, whose fortune was founded on a hair straightener. She had
been a scrubwoman and a laundress.
It was estimated in 1978 that 50.4 per cent of the United States'
250,000 millionaires are in fact millionairesses.

Wealth and Poverty ■ 493

Walker's business
employed over 3,000
Black women. Founded in 1905,
its products are still sold today.

We'll forgive Mr. Guiness for not being aware of
Sistuh MAKEDA, Queen of Sheba, back in the 900's B.C. Her
sharp business acumen made her exceedingly rich, possibly
the richest African monarch ever.

Slave BIDDY MASON won
her freedom, then made a
fortune in real estate in early
Los Angeles.

T.C.B. means Tough, Creative Bargaining

In Africa, women control the marketplace, setting prices and trade, much like Makeda did. Women in polygamous marriages might negotiate a good business set-up in exchange for congenial acceptance of a new wife.

Carribean women have made the "higgler" an institution—the grass-roots businesswoman hawking her home-grown produce and notions.

A banking system exists through-out the world—"partners" in Jamaica, "susu" in Trinidad—where women combine their savings regu-larly, then each "takes a draw" to start a business, schooling, etc. Newly freed slaves in the U.S. devel-oped it into the Freedman's bank system when Whites would not make property loans to Blacks.

MAGGIE LENA WALKER turned a community's sick and burial fund into a thriving bank, becoming the U.S.'s first BW bank president.

RACHEL PRINGLE, Barbados' first hotel owner, in 1781. History records that the son of King George III and his brawling friends tore up the place and kicked her out on the street. But she was cool. The Prince was billed, and paid for, an extravagant remodeling job.

T.C.B. mean's Takin' Care of the **B**rothers and **S**istuhs.

The Western media project the BW as dependent on government and Other's benevolence for survival. But the BWn has always **initiated** actions to take care of herself and her own.

Madame Walker, a woman with no formal education, helped fund Mary McLeod Bethune's school and scholarships at Tuskeegee Institute. She gave cash bonuses to her agents to be used for community upliftment.

In the 1800's women in Brazil formed Boa Morte, a secret society that fought slavery by buying the freedom of female slaves. In the U.S., a former slave, JANE MINOR, saved her money and, one by one, bought up to 15 other slaves and set them free.

SLAVE RESALE SHOP

Camille Cosby, with her husband "The Cos,"in 1988 made the largest single contribution ever given to a Black college: $20 million.

T.C.B. means doing your J.O.B.

Black women are the hardest working women in the world!

Madagascar woman

"At six in the morning
through the streets of the city
a voice rings in the air;
the cry of the vendor,
   Marimorena.

. . .

When a man of the press
passes by you. . .
he pretends not to hear;
so that when you can no
   no longer
peddle the paper which
   he writes
you will be without a crumb,
and no one will subscribe
   to you.

. . .

For four cents a paper,
Marimorena,
the cloth of her shroud."

Virginia Brindis de Salas
(Uruguay)

Traditional work has been as farmers, hunters, healers, housekeepers and dressmakers, midwives and teachers.

Traditional because for so long these were the only occupations available to her.

I Sell the Shadow to Support the Substance.

SOJOURNER TRUTH.

SUSIE KING TAYLOR, an ex slave, served as a volunteer nurse in the Civil War.

The U.S. Army recruited African-American nurses for the Spanish-American War (1898) because it was believed their race made them immune to typhoid fever.

By 1990 BWn comprised almost 5% of the U.S. Armed Forces, trading the nurse's cap for a **combat** helmet.

165

"The Lady Marshall." In 1987 three Black women in Nicaragua became the first local women to own their own fishing boat.

As the principal food gatherer, she has learned the nature of plants, herbs and roots, which made her the planet's first herbalists, first doctors.

She's served as **unpaid** mediator, strategist, cook.

Tagesablauf einer afrikanischen   **AFRICAN WOMEN**

und einer europäischen Frau   **EUROPEAN WOMEN**

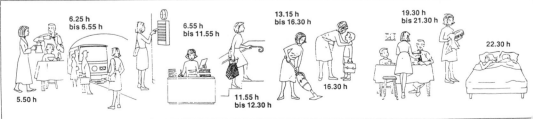

A UNESCO analysis, 1975

Wasn't there any way she could make things easier?? Well, yes:

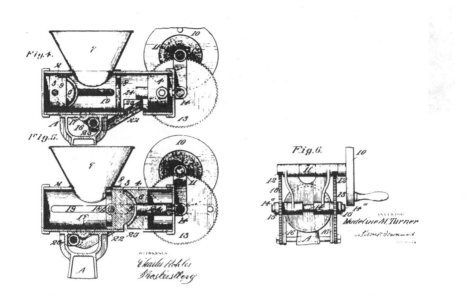

In 1916 MADELINE TURNER invented one of the first mechanized fruit juicers.

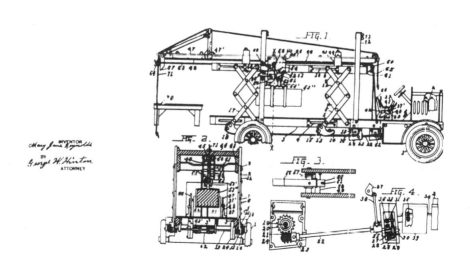

MARY JANE REYNOLDS invented a hoisting and loading mechanism in 1920 that gets heavy loads onto trucks with ease.

In developing countries the BW is the least likely to be trained for industrial and high-tech jobs, earns approximately one-half the income of Black males and as little as 1% of the income of White males.

"[In Tanzania] for African women in self-employment, access to capital and accumulation are further limited by...government policies that favored the development of Tanzanian Asians as a commercial class... The segregated Asian schools specialized in commercial courses."

> Willene A. Johnson,
> "Women And Self-Employment
> In Urban Tanzania."   (1971)

"My life is but a dirty penny
that is only valued because
it is the only one
My life is but a ten rand note
that can be used only because
there may be change"

> Zindzi Mandela
> (South Africa)

Even in wealthy U.S.A., BWn heading households earn only one-third of what their White counterparts earn, according to 1988 census stats.

THE FIRST NEGRO
HALL OF FAME

BESSIE COLEMAN, refused flying privileges in the U.S., trained in France and in 1922 became the world's first BW licensed pilot.

DR. MAE C. JEMISON, the world's first Black female astronaut (USA), trained for five years before making her first shuttle space flight in the Endeavor, in September, 1992.

ULAMAE MARGIE SCOTT, born in Russia, joined the famed Bolshoi Ballet in the 1940's when she was 8, and became its first BW ballerina and choreographer.

SURYA BONALY, French figure skater, in 1991 became the first BW European Figure Skating Champion.

BARBARA C. HARRIS, (the Right Reverend), beat down 2000 years of resistance, becoming the first woman Bishop in the Episcopal church. (1989).

"We specialize in the wholly impossible."

Nannie Helen Burroughs, (1909) (USA)
Nat'l Trade and Professional School for Women and Girls

"Someone out there is blowin' his mind Keeping track of the First Negro in every line."

She has served as the culture bearer, breaking
social taboos and racial barriers with a song.

"Tonight Only"
Cuban Conductor
"TANIA LEON"
and the
Hieroglyphic Art Ensemble

batik art by NIKE TWINS SEVEN SEVEN (Nigeria)

T.C.B. is notifying the world about what's on her mind.

The BW can claim writing as a profession going back to SAPPHO, Greece's gifted aristocrat (600's B.C.), described by other writers as small, dark, Ethiopian, and "not beautiful."

Who wrote that?

URSULA
Maria Firmino dos Reis
PRESENÇA/MinC/PRÓ-MEMÓRIA
INSTITUTO NACIONAL DO LIVRO
Coleção Resgate v.12

Brazil's MARIA F. dos REIS, author of the novel *Ursula*, and the USA's HARRIET WILSON, author of *Our Nig*, are the first BWn known to publish novels, both in 1859.

"The Black Woman is both a ship and a safe harbor."

Novelist Toni Morrison

Afro-Russian journalist YELENA KHANGA, the only Black journalist to cover the historic 1988 Reagan/Gorbachev summit.

"I am Black by birth, and Russian by soul."

173

VIRGINIA BRINDIS de SALAS, poet-journalist of Uruguay writing about the harshness of women's lives, is among the first Afro-Latin women to receive literary acclaim.

"I go every-where without hesitation. Hallelujah!"

LOUISE BENNETT, Jamaica's foremost poet and folklorist, has popularized Jamaican dialect in her writings since the 1930's.

**"Neck an neck and foot an foot wid man
She buckle hole her own;
While man call her 'so-so rib'
Oman a tun back bone!"**

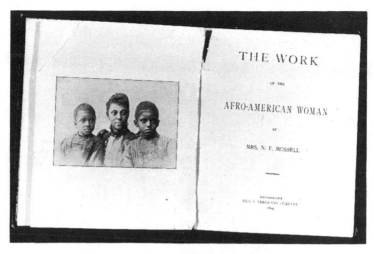

The work of journalists was documented
by Mrs. N.E. Mossell in 1894 .

"A woman said to me
      T'other day . . .
I read one of your poems
      About women,
I thought it very good
But
It didn't say that you
      were BLACK

Now I meet you and
      see that you
      are BLACK
I wonder
Why you wrote the poem?

Do <u>they</u> think
      we spend
      our whole lives
            being BLACK
                  for <u>them</u>?"

Bobbi Sykes (Australia)

"*Woman to woman now, we tell our beads
on the worn rosary of years
together in the same slant of light
No longer clay and potter,
we are what we have made each other,
your mark indelibly on me
as mine on you...*

Naomi Long Madgett (USA)

Old problems repackaged trail the
BW into the 21st century, challenging
the survival of the living trinity:
body, mind and spirit.

Divas Don't Die. Still, some of the Sistuhs are no longer with us.

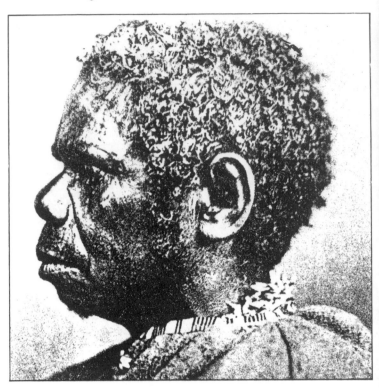

TRUGANINNI, "the last living Tasmanian," photographed in 1864. This South Pacific race of 20 thousand (approximately 8000 BWn) was exterminated by the British in only 75 years.

Divas Don't Die. Still, some of the Sistuhs live under the threat of decimation.

BWn face long-term, carefully plotted programs of "de-population," initiated by the Western world's leading governments, against people of color in areas (Africa in particular) where there are natural resources needed by the rest of the world.

National Security Study Memorandum 200

October, 1974

TO: The Secretary of State
The Secretary of Defense
Director of Central Intelligence
The Administrator of the Agency for International Development

SUBJECT: De-Population of Third World States

Reduction of the rate of population in these states is a matter of vital U.S. national security. The U.S. economy will require large and increasing amounts of minerals from abroad, especially from less developed countries. Wherever a lessening of population can increase the prospect for such stability population policy becomes relevant to resources, supplies and to the economic interests of the United States.

Divas Don't Die.
Still, some of the mothers are no longer giving birth. Forced sterilization is rampant. The new fetal technology is mind-blowing!

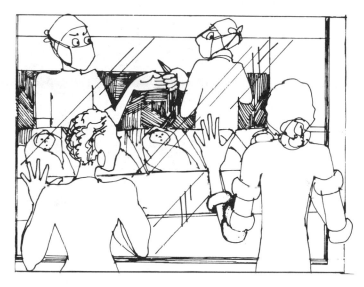

QUESTION:

"Can they use this technology to wipe out races or classes of people?"

ANSWER:

"With it, they can kill the un-born child they don't like, so the control will be in the hands of somebody else."

Reproductive Health Workshop, U.N. Decade Of The Woman Conference, Nairobi, 1985

Divas Don't Die. Still some of the
Sistuhs are forced to master Solitaire.

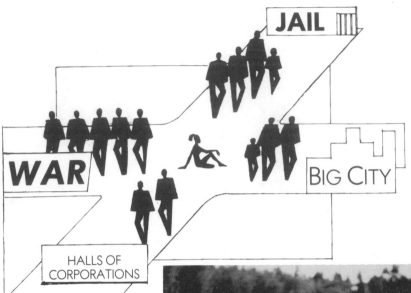

JAIL

WAR

BIG CITY

HALLS OF
CORPORATIONS

Divas Don't Die. Even
though some of the
Sistuhs have been
worked to death.

Some women
spend an estimated
one-third of their day
securing **water** for the
family—finding it,
walking to it, lifting it
from wells, scraping it
from riverbeds,
hauling it, using it
and storing it.

Women are still purchased to increase a man's labor force, via marriage. The "dowry" or "lobolo" compensates the family for giving up part of **its** labor force.

I thought I lived with trouble
Til it camped outside your door...

Divas Don't Die. Somehow they live through that which should surely kill them.

"An old woman like me, 60 or 65 years old, is forced to have sex with her son or grandson. This is what makes us hate them. In some areas... they've cut off young girls' hands, accusing them of providing food for SWAPO."

Rosa Carina Tavares, speaking in 1987 on South Africa's UNITA forces' war against Black Angolans.

"Mr. Close-Friend-of-the-Family Pays A Visit
Whilst Everyone Else is Out," by Sonia Boyce (Britian)

"So much violence against women acts itself out in the area of the sexual. The man sees himself as the subject, the woman as the object, and that object cannot have her own agenda. If sexual desire can be controlled, then so can dreaming and the desire to be something."

Cheryl Chisholm (USA)

Divas Don't Die. They live in the war zone of **Control,** the bones scattered across the battlefield.

Rape is global. In the "civilized" United States, a woman is raped approximately every 7 minutes, and an average of four per day are killed.

Woman beating is global.

"It's difficult to draw the line between custom and abuse.... In Trinidad there is the unspoken belief that abuse is part of the 'for better or for worse' marriage package.... So we are concerned about how women perpetuate the problem."

Eunice Gittens,
Rape Crisis Center,
Port-of-Spain, Trinidad

Forced prostitution is global. Women surrendering their bodies for a meal, for the job which feeds their children.

Clitoridectomy—the practice of cutting a woman's clitoris to lessen sexual desire—is global, but done primarily in African and Arab nations, justified by religion and tradition. **Women perpetuate clitoridectomy.** This life threatening surgery is endorsed by men, but performed by women on women.

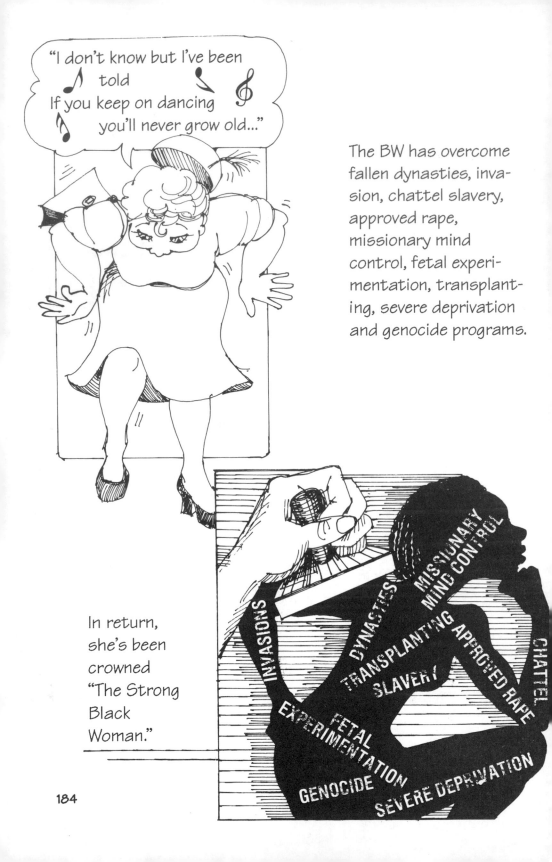

"I don't know but I've been told ♪ If you keep on dancing you'll never grow old..."

The BW has overcome fallen dynasties, invasion, chattel slavery, approved rape, missionary mind control, fetal experimentation, transplanting, severe deprivation and genocide programs.

In return, she's been crowned "The Strong Black Woman."

184

"When people talk about the 'strength' of
black women… they ignore the reality
that to be strong in the face of oppression is not the
same as overcoming oppression, that endurance is
not to be confused with transformation."

Bell Hooks, *Ain't I A Woman* (USA)

Divas Don't Die. They learn to love themselves.

Today more concentration is focused on BWn
learning about each other than ever before—
woman to woman, country to country,
ancestor to ancestor.

"I HAVE COME TO KNOW MYSELF AND HAVE GATHERED MYSELF FROM EVERYWHERE"

Uh-oh!

Divas Don't Die.
Divas don't die. They are the living stream,
the divine and destined continuum of Black
Women on the planet, connected to all who
preceded them and all who follow.

"With all the reversals...we have learned that
black is the beginning of every thing. It was
black in the universe before the sun. . . . ;

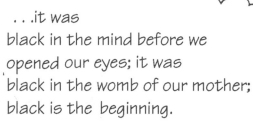

. . .it was
black in the mind before we
opened our eyes; it was
black in the womb of our mother;
black is the beginning.

And if we are the beginning
we will be forever."

Sonia Sanchez
homegirls and handgrenades (USA)

Ashay...
Amen...
Asim...
Axé... Eshi...
Saya...
And so it is.

SELECTED

photo: Gordon Parks

BIBLIOGRAPHY

Ansa, Tina McElroy. *Baby of the Family*. Harcourt, Brace, Jovanovich, 1989. (novel)

Black Science Activity Books. *Salute to Black Women Inventors*. Chicago: Chandler/White Publ., 1990. (for young readers)

Blakely, Allison. *Russia and the Negro: Blacks in Russian History and Thought*. Washington: Howard University Press, 1986.

Busby, Margaret. *Daughters of Africa: An International Anthology of Words and Writing by Women of African Descent from the Ancient Egyptian to the Present*. London: Jonathan Cage, 1992.

Clifton, Lucille. *Good Woman: Poems and a Memoir, 1969-1980*. Brockport, N.Y.: Boa Editions, Ltd., 1987; orig. Reed, Cannon & Johnson, 1978.

Cobham, Rhonda and Collins, Merle. *Watchers & Seekers: Creative Writing by Black Women*. London: The Women's Press Ltd., 1987. New York: Peter Bedrick, 1988. (British women writers)

Davies, David. *The Last of the Tasmanians*. New York: Harper & Row, 1974. (on extinction of an Aboriginal tribe)

Davies, Miranda. *Third World-Second Sex: Women's Struggles and National Liberation*. London: Zed Press, 1983.

Gabre-Tsadick, Marta. *Marta: A Refugee's Story*. London: Triangle, 1983. (Ethiopia)

Giddings, Paula. *When and Where I Enter: The Impact of Black Women On Race In America*. New York: William Morrow, 1984.

Haniff, Nesha Z. *Blaze a Fire: Significant Contributions of Caribbean Women*. Toronto: Sister Vision, 1988.

Head, Bessie. *Meru*. Oxford: Heinemann International, 1971. (South African novel)

Hooks, Bell. *Ain't I a Woman: Black Women and Feminism*. Boston: South End Press, 1981.

Igus, Toyomi; Freeman, Veronica; Patrick, Diane; Wesley, Valerie Wilson. *Book of Black Heroes: Great Women in the Struggle*. Orange, New Jersey: Just Us Book, 1991.

Lorde, Audre. *Zami: A New Spelling of My Name*. Persephone Press/The Crossing Press, 1982. ("a biomythology")

Malveaux, Julianne M. and Simms, Margaret C. *Slipping Through The Cracks: The Status of Black Women*. New Brunswick: Transaction Publ., 1986.

Mandela, Winnie. *Part of My Soul Went With Him*. New York: W.W. Norton, 1984.

Morejon, Nancy. *Where the Island Sleeps Like a Wing*. Black Scholar Press, 1985; originally published: Havana: Cuban National Center for Author's Rights. (poetry)

Nunez, Benjamin. *Dictionary of Afro-Latin Civilization*. Connecticut: Greenwood Press, 1980.

Oguntoye, Katharina; Opitz, May; Schultz, Dagmar. *Showing Our Colors: Afro-German Women Speak Out*. Amherst: University of Massachusetts Press, 1992; originally published: Berlin: Farbe Bekennen, 1986.

Olsen, Anne and Seager, Joni. *Women in the World: An International Atlas*. New York: Simon & Schuster, 1987

Rashidi, Runoko and Van Sertima, Ivan. *African Presence In Early Asia*. New Brunswick: Transaction Books, 1984.

Robinson, Beverly. *Jemima, Eliza and Edith: You Have Nothing to be Ashamed Of*. Oakland: Regent Press, 1993.

Smith, Shirley C. and Sykes, Bobbi. *Mum Shirl*. Victoria, Australia: Heinemann Publ., 1981. (Aboriginal autobiography)

BIBLIOGRAPHY

Steady, Filomina Chioma. *The Black Woman Cross-Culturally*. Rochester, Vermont: Schenkman Books, 1981.

Sterling, Dorothy. We Are Your Sisters: *Black Women in the Nineteenth Century*. New York: W.W. Norton, 1984.

Sweetman, David. *Women Leaders in African History*. Oxford: Heinemann International, 1984. Lorde, Audre. *Zami: A New Spelling of My Name*. Persephone Press/The Crossing Press, 1982. ("a biomythology")

United Nations Center Against Apartheid; International Defence and Aid Fund for Southern Africa (IDAF). *Women Under Apartheid*. London, 1981. (photo essay)

Van Sertima, Ivan. *Black Women in Antiquity*. New Brunswick: Transaction Books, 1984, 1992.

Van Sertima, Ivan. *They Came Before Columbus: African Presence in Ancient America*. New York: Random House, 1976.

Wells, Ida B. *Crusade For Justice; Autobiography of Ida B. Wells*. Chicago: University of Chicago Press, 1970.

Williams, Chancellor. *Destruction of Black Civilization: 4500 B.C. to 2000 A. D.* Dubuque, Iowa: Kendall/Hunt, 1971; Third World Press, 1987.

FILMS & VIDEOTAPES

Afram, Silvana. *Black Women of Brazil*. Brazil, 1986. Distributed by Women Make Movies, New York.

Blackwood, Maureen. *Perfect Image?* Britain, 1988. Distributed by Black Film Institute, London and Third World Newsreel, New York.

Chenzira, Ayoka. *Hairpiece: A Film for Nappy-Headed People*. USA, 1985. Distributed by Women Make Movies, New York.

Dash, Julie. *Daughters of the Dust*. USA, 1992. Distributed by Kino Films, New York.

Davis, Elmina. *Omega Rising: Women of the Rastafari*. 1988

Griffin, Ada and Parkerson, Michelle. *Litany for Survival: The Life and Work of Audre Lorde*. USA, 1993. Third World Newsreel, New York.

Hondo, Med. *Sarrounia*. Mauritania/Burkina Faso, 1987. Distributed by M.H. Films, Paris.

Milwe, Bea with National Black Women's Health Project. *It's Up To Us*. USA, 1986. Distributed by Women Make Movies, New York. (U.N. Decade of the Woman Nairobi Conference)

Mawuru, Godwin. *Neria*. Zimbabwe, 1990. Distributed by DSR, Columbia, Maryland. Milwe, Bea with National Black Women's Health Project. *It's Up To Us*. USA, 1986. Distributed by Women Make Movies, New York. (U.N. Decade of the Woman Nairobi Conference)

Morgan, Jenny with Organization of Angolan Women. *Angola e a Nossa Terra* (Angola Is Our Country). 1988. Distributed Women Make Movies, New York.

Sharp, Saundra. *Picking Tribes*. USA, 1984. Distributed by Women Make Movies, New York.

Sissolo, Cheick Oumar. *Finzan: A Dance for the Heroes*. Mali, 1990. Distributed by California Newsreel, San Francisco.

Soloman, Frances-Anne and Lewis, Ingrid. *I Is a Long-Memoried Woman*. England, 1990. Distributed by Women Make Movies, New York. (based on the poems of Grace Nichols, Guyana/Britain)

CREDITS

p6 Julie Dash, *Daughters of the Dust* (Julie Dash, P.O. Box 13938, Atlanta, Georgia 30324)

WHERE DID SHE COME FROM? (AND THEN WHERE DID SHE GO?)

p16 L. Carrington Goodrich, *A Short History of the Chinese People* (New York: Harper & Brothers, 1943)

p21 Joseph John Williams, *Whence The 'Black Irish' Of Jamaica* (New York: Dial Press, 1932)

p22 Brunold Springer, *Racial Mixture As The Basic Principle of Life* (New York: New York Times Book Review, @1940)

p26 C. Madang, *Africa Magazine* (1976)

p28 William Loren Katz, *Black Indians* (New York: Atheneum, 1986)

p29 Mary Seacole, *Wonderful Adventures of Mary Seacole In Many Lands* (London: J. Blackwood, 1857)

p30 Doris Reiprich, Erika Ngambi ul Kuo, *Farbe Bekennen (Showing Our Colors)* (Massachusetts: University of Mass. Press, 1991)

p34 Claude McKay, *Home To Harlem* (New York: Harper Row, 1928)

NAMES BY WHICH SHE IS KNOWN

p36 Archie Weller, *Paperbark: Black Australian Writings* (University of Queensland Press, 1990)

THE BEAUTY BANK

p48 Chikh Anta Diop, *African Origin of Civilization* (New York: L. Hill, 1974)

p53 Savina J. Teubal, *Hagar The Egyptian* (San Francisco: HarperCollins, 1990)

p54 George Washington Cable, *The Grandissimes* (Georgia: University of Georgia Press, 1860)

p57 William Faulkner, *Go Down Moses* (New York: Random House, 1942)

p58 *Public Relations Review* (Fall 1990)

p62 Mary Helen Washington, *Sturdy Black Bridges* (New York: Doubleday, 1979)

p63 Henry D. Spalding, Editor, *Encyclopedia of Black Folklore And Humor* (New York: Jonathan David Publishers, Inc., 1978)

p69 Paddy Calistro, *Los Angeles Times Magazine* (1989)

p70 Ntozke Shange, *for colored girls who have considered suicide when the rainbow is enuf* (New York: Bantam Doubleday, 1979)

MADONNAS OR MADAMS?

p76 J. A. Rogers, *Sex and Race, Vol. I* (New York: J.A. Rogers Publishers, 1967)

p78 James A. Preston, editor, *Mother Worship* (Chapel Hill: University of N. Carolina Press, 1982)

p80 Ivan Van Sertima, *Women In Antiquity* (New Jersey: Transaction Books, 1984)

p81 Winthrop D. Jordan, *White Over Black* (New York: W.W. Norton, 1977)

WITCHES, WIVES, & WARRIORS

p90 Susan L. Taylor, *Essence Magazine*, "I Will" (1988)

p92 Marc Edmund Jones, *Occult Philosophy* (Sabian Publisher, 1948)

p93 Zora Neale Hurston, *Dust Tracks On the Road* (New York: HarperPerrenial, 1991)

p94 Elaine Armour, "Woman as Goddess, Priestess, Whore" audiotape (Aquarian Spiritual Center, Los Angeles)

p95 Bernice Reagon, "B'Lieve I'll Run On See What The End's Gonna Be" album (SWITR P.O. Box 54245 Washington, D. C. 20032)

p96 Alan Lomax and Raoul Abdul, editors, *3000 Years Of Black Poetry* (New York: Dodd, Mead, 1970)

p99 Lillian Smith, *Killers Of The Dream* (New York: W.W. Norton, 1949, revised 1961)

p102 Asa Hilliard III, Larry Williams, Nia Damali, editors, *The Teachings of Ptah Hotep* (Atlanta: Blackwood Press, @1987)

p103 James Brunson, author; Runoko Rashidi and Ivan Van Sertima, editors, *African Presence In Early Asia* (New Jersey: Transaction Books, 1985)

p103 Catherine Clinton, *The Plantation Mistress* (New York: Pantheon, 1982)

MOVERS & SHAKERS

p139 Shirley Chisolm, *Unbought and Unbossed* (Boston: Houghton-Mifflin 1970)

p141 Carolina Marie de Jesus, *Child of the Dark* (New York: Dutton, 1963: Livaria Francisca Alves, Brazil, 1960)

p148 Gloria Gayles, *Sturdy Black Bridges* (New York: Doubleday, 1979)

p148 Jean Carey Bond, *Essence Magazine*, "From The Bottom Up" (1985)

p155 Safiya Henderson Holmes, *Madness And A Bit of Hope* (New York: Harlem River Press, 1991)

TAKIN' CARE OF BIZNESS

p157 Brother Ojenke (3736 1/2 W. Slauson, Los Angeles, CA 90043)

p168 Simms and Malveaux, editors, *Slipping Through The Cracks* (New Jersey: Transaction Publication, 1986)

p168 Zindzi Mandela, *Black As I Am* (Los Angeles: Guild Tutor Press, 1978)

p174 Morris and Kingston, editors, *Selected Poems* (Jamaica: Sangster's Bookstores, 1982)

p175 Bobbi Sykes, *Love Poems and Other Revolutionary Actions* (Australia: The Saturday Center, 1979)

p175 Aretha Franklin "Respect" by Otis Redding, East-Time-Redwal-BMI/ from "Aretha in Paris" (Atlantic, 1968)

DIVAS DON'T DIE

p177 Naomi Long Madgett, *Sage Magazine* (Detroit: Lotus Press, 1987)

p181 Rosa Carina Tavares, *Angola Is My Country* (film)

p186 Sonia Sanchez, *homegirls & handgrenades* (New York: Thunders Mouth Press, 1985) p15 Dravidian woman: collection of Runoko Rashidi

p21 Amanda Cash: collection of Mark Greenfield

p23 Tsan Merritt Poree, Elizabeth Cohen-Johnston: collection of Tsan Merritt Poree

p25 "The Assiento" London, 1713, p38 "Coal Black Rose", 1831, p82 New Orleans Blue Book, 1908: The Charles Blockson Collection, Temple University

p30 Afro-German Women: Fare Bekennen (Showing Our Colors), University of Massachusettes Press, Amherst

p32 Brazil editorial poster on assimilation: courtesy Regina Dominquez, I.B.A.S.E., Brazil

p34 African woman, pregnant nude belly: Jacqueline Alexander, Jacqueline Alexander & Co., 4834 St. Elmo Drive, Los Angeles, CA 90019

p54 Coon Coon Apricot ad, p56 mammy images: cans, products, p58 earliest Aunt Jemima (Nancy Green), p66 Niggerhair Tobacco tin: Ethnic Notions Exhibition Catalog, Janette Faulkner Collection

p57 German advertisements: collection of Natalie Asfaha

p60 Nigerian Barbie Doll: Mattel Toys

p61 Coco-cola advertising tray, "The Wedding": collection of Malinda Saunders

p65 Madame C. J. Walker product hair ad, p67 Madame C. J. Walker's "Tan-Off": collection of Stanley Nelson

p71 Cheryl Tatum-Tandia: Charles Ford, photographer; Eric Steele, attorney

p72 Patti LaBelle: collection of Rudy Calvo

p82 Black Hawaiian Monarchs, wives, p116 Lydia Lili'uokalani, Hawaii: Richard A. Wisniewski, *Black Hawaiian Monarchs and Their Palaces*, Pacific Basin Enterprises, Box 8924, Honolulu, Hawaii 96830

p83 Cleopatra by Earl Sweeting: collection of Ora Sweeting

p104 Amenirdas I presents bowl of wine to Amon, 25th Dyn: *Image of Blacks In Western Art, Vol. 1* page 113, fig. 106 (Harvard University Press, Cambridge)

p105 Amy Jacques Garvey, *Essence Magazine: Amy in UNIA Uniform*, by Jean Carey Bond, May 1985

p105 Nelson & Winnie Mandela (nose-to-nose, 1959): *Part Of My Soul Went With Him* (New York: W.W. Norton, 1984)

p105 Josina Machel: *Makers Of Modern Africa: Profiles In History* (London: Africa Journal Ltd., Africa Books, 1981)

p107 Funerary sculpture of Amenhotep & Tiye: Edward Scobie, *Black Women in Antiquity*

p107 Nefertiti and Akhenaten: Aldred, *Akhenaten and Nefertiti*

p112 Dahomey Women archer, single breast: E. Jefferson Murphy, *History of African Civilization* (New York: World Publishers, 1963)

p114 YYA ASANTEWA, Gold Coast/Ghana 1900: *Women Leaders In African History* (Oxford: Sweetman Heinemann International)

p120 Sandanista soldier: Ron Wilkins, photographer

p138 Marta Gabre-Tsadick: *1990 Calendar, Distinguished Black Women*, published by Black Women In Sisterhood For Action

p141 Addis Ababa woman cooking, 1987: Saundra Sharp, photographer

p141 Carolina Maria de Jesus: Saundra Sharp, *Child Of The Dark*

p143 Mum Shirl's jail pass (Australia): Bobbi Sykes, *Mum Shirl* (Australia)

p144 SACTU labor group, South Africa: *Women Under Apartheid* (S. Africa: IDAF)

p144 Trinidad NCWS poster, early 1900's, p146 Elma Francois: Rhoda Reddock, *Elma Francois* (London: New Beacon Books, 1988)

p146 Lillian Ngoyi: *Makers Of Modern Africa* (edited 1981)

p146 Albertina Sisulu: *Africa Report: "Albertina Sisulu: The Work Of Women"* by Margaret Novickik, Nov./Dec. 1992

p146 The Red Record: Ida B. Wells, *The Red Record*

p146 Beulah Mae Donald: *Essence*, Oct. 1988, Dwight Carter, photographer

p164 Madagascar woman carrying bricks: United Nations Photo Library, #140-097, I. Rajonina, photographer

p171 Nike Twins Seven Seven: collection of Betty LaDuke

p180 "Water Is Vital For Life"/Ethiopia 1983: courtesy United Nations, #153487, Peter Magubane, photographer

p187 Muslim Women: Gordon Parks

"listen children
keep this in the place
you have for keeping
always
keep it all ways

we have never hated black

listen
we have been ashamed
hopeless   tired   mad
but always
all ways
we loved us

we have always loved each other
children   all ways

pass it on"

Lucille Clifton (USA)